A BOOK ON

FEAR

ON | FEELING SAFE IN A CHALLENGING WORLD

LAWRENCE DOOCHIN

I am deeply grateful to my wife, Janice, and our children, Sarah, Thomas, David, Hannah, and our son-in-law Matt, for loving and accepting me unconditionally. Thank you for not giving up on me and being there through many years of depression and fear. You have kept me grounded and helped me to remember what is important.

To my good friend Lily Whitehawk, I am very grateful for your guidance, teaching, and love. Thank you for being the one to tell me that I was supposed to write the book now instead of later.

And words cannot express my gratitude for God, who I love with all of my heart and soul. God is the source of my inspiration and writing and the one who gives my life purpose and joy.

CONTENTS

—

PREFACE

Most people who write a nonfiction book are experts on the topic they are writing about. I am an expert on fear. You may find this somewhat unusual, or perhaps amusing. In order to be an expert on something, you really need to have repeatedly experienced it in real life, because learning about it in school isn't the same. I have experienced and released a great deal of fear. This isn't something I would have chosen, but in a strange sort of way it has been a gift for me as it allowed me to deeply know myself as I worked through this fear. And my experience has equipped me to write this book as a way of helping others who are experiencing fear.

I wouldn't call myself a master of fear yet, because it still pops its head up to remind me of situations that don't serve me. Like a good friend, it will continue to do that until its messages are no longer needed. My suggestion and hope for all of us is that we become experts on fear and learn how to master it. For if we don't, it will be the master of us.

Unfortunately, this is what is currently happening for many people, especially when they have never encountered something so life-altering as the changes the coronavirus crisis has brought. (I write this preface in late March 2020.) Each of us can feel the shock of events changing rapidly and being out of our control, similar to the shock were our house to burn down or were a loved one to become sick and we couldn't do anything about it. We are on a collective journey, yet we don't know where that journey is taking us, and this can only engender great fear.

In order to heal something, we first have to acknowledge it exists. Fear is like the emperor who had no clothes or the elephant in the room. It's pretty darn evident that we currently exist in an atmosphere of rampant fear, but few are talking about it in any meaningful way — at least, not in a way that truly helps us come up with a solution. And I don't mean a solution like eradicating the virus.

After we acknowledge our fear, we can begin to seek its source within us and release what we falsely believe. The "outer" source is only a trigger for other fears we hold. If we don't heal the real source of our fear, it becomes irrelevant what the "outer" trigger is, because we will always be subject to fear. When the coronavirus is eradicated or wanes, there will always be something, globally or individually, that will substitute as the next trigger for our fear, even though we "fixed" the last one.

The situation we find ourselves in both individually and collectively isn't random. We are in a time of great change. As is always the case, we have a choice. We can choose to resist what is happening, which puts us in more fear, or we can choose to see it from a much higher perspective and trust that there is a greater good occurring for us and the world, even if it appears and feels very differently. Taking the latter perspective allows us to flow with the river of life and not fight the scenery changes which are quickly being presented to us.

This crisis has made us highly aware that we are one humanity. Regardless of the level of our wealth or status, nationality or political persuasion, religion, age, race, or gender, we are all experiencing this crisis together, and this is a powerful realization that can be comforting and lead to empathy.

I know well that the energy of fear doesn't feel good. Thankfully, it's not how we are meant to live. My hope is that by the end of the book, you will see that there is a permanent way out of fear. Even if many others remain in fear and the collective trend line stays one of fear, this doesn't have to be your personal experience.

A Book On Fear will help you achieve this by giving you tools and awarenesses to see where your fear comes from. This will enable you to be cognizant of it whenever it arises, but you won't become attached to or drawn into the fear of others or what is occurring. *A Book On Fear* may also help you to see the potential gifts that can come out of a crisis. By the end of the book, you may actually be grateful for the lessons and gifts that fear has brought, and you may call it your friend.

In gratitude,

> *"The only thing
> we have to fear is
> fear itself."*

PRESIDENT FRANKLIN
DELANO ROOSEVELT

ONE

WHAT IS FEAR?

THE FIRST STEP IN CORRECTING ANYTHING IS IDENTIFYING THE source. For instance, if we have water pooling in our house, we have to find the source of the leak. The same process applies to fear. Once we determine where it is coming from, we can find a solution.

The issue with fear is that it often masks itself really well. Some people don't realize they are in fear and just feel a general uneasiness. For others of us, we know it's fear, but even in these cases, we often identify fear with something outside of us. This can take many forms such as fear over losing our job, not having enough money, getting older, and losing our health in general or through exposure to a pandemic. It can include fear over failed relationships or not finding a significant other, not keeping up with the neighbors, or something like being bombed by another country. As we will discuss more extensively in a later chapter, our fears are almost always tied to something in the future and based on a random and often illogical assumption that a certain scenario or event *could* happen.

What we often miss is the fear that comes up from our subconscious and is created by our belief system, and these types of fears are interlinked with and underpin the more obvious outer ones above. Some of these fears can include fear of the unknown, not being in control, not being lovable, not being good enough, and not living up to other's or our own expectations. Many of us hold a subconscious fear of being judged or ridiculed — we have a fear of what others *might* think about us. There is also a powerful fear of a higher power and what will happen when death comes. Additionally, many collective and family fears are likely inherited from our ancestors. For instance, studies of descendants of Holocaust and Civil War survivors have pointed to intergenerational trauma being passed down through the DNA.

Some fears are unique to us, while others are held by a large majority. Collective fear is what we experience together as part of one humanity, like the fear of dying. The coronavirus crisis has brought fear of the unknown to the forefront for all of us because we don't know what the future will look like.

As opposed to love and gratitude, fear is divisive and contracting, and there are often other negative beliefs around it such as jealousy, resentment, bitterness, self-pity, anger, and pride. Fear makes us not trust our fellow human beings or any kind of higher power.

When we are in fear, we try to control people and situations. Fear causes people to act in ways that are completely counter to their true nature such as misuse of power, overaccumulation of wealth and resources, subjugation of Mother Nature, being a rude and non-empathetic person, and traits such as impatience. This is why we have the world you see today.

There is nothing wrong with us when we have fear. It's something that virtually everyone in a human body has to face. Sometimes fear is good. It warns us not to do something that could endanger us, like walking fast on ice, jumping off a bridge into a river on a dare, or taking a hallucinogenic drug. But most of the time the fear is coming up as a pointer to tell us what's false within us that needs addressing.

As the FDR quote hints at, most of us live in fear of our fear. It is our running from and stuffing and being scared of the fear that is the problem. Anything in us that we try to ignore or push away only becomes stronger as we have an innate drive to return to a recognition that we are whole and complete. Our fear is just knocking at our inner door to get our attention, just as a friend would knock on our door if he saw that our house were ablaze.

All fear stems from attaching our identity to something false. This is why we can't get rid of the fear by changing the outer circumstances. Thus, we don't alleviate fear through the same mechanism that created it. For instance, if we are in a company that has had major layoffs and we fear that this will happen to us, we can take another job, but this only *appears* to alleviate our fear. The same thing can happen in the new company.

A Japanese proverb states, "Fear is only as deep as the mind allows." We can only address and release the fear at the level at which it's being created, which is in the subconscious and our belief system. Fortunately, our beliefs are malleable. Unfortunately, many of us in great fear hold on to our beliefs as if we would experience a thousand small deaths if we let them evolve — which at some level we would. However, this is how we grow and what we are being offered an opportunity to do during this powerful time.

Since fear is a belief, our next few chapters explore how both our individual and collective belief systems were created. Once we understand why we do the things we do and react as we do, we can choose to change our beliefs to better reflect who we are and who we want to be. Then we can release fear for good.

MAIN TAKEAWAY

Fear is a belief, and like all beliefs, it can be changed.

 What do you fear the most? What belief did that fear spring from?

> "Money has never made man happy, nor will it. There is nothing in its nature to produce happiness. The more of it one has the more one wants."

BENJAMIN FRANKLIN

SOCIETAL
BELIEF SYSTEMS

WHEN WE ARE TAUGHT THAT WE SHOULD HAVE SOMETHING or achieve a certain thing and we aren't yet there, this will automatically engender fear and anxiety in us until we believe we reach these goals.

We have been told to strive for the American dream, assured that this is the key to happiness. The American dream includes accumulation of a large amount of wealth and status, a respected career, and well-educated children.

Many of us achieve the American dream but then discover that it isn't enough, because "enough" can never be defined. So we strive to add more, accumulating more than we could possibly need. When we strive for something false, we can never reach the destination. We live our life as "when." I will be happy *when* I have this amount of money, *when* I am VP of the company, *when* I have my soulmate. The Dalai Lama said, "When you are discontent, you always want more, more, more. Your desire can never be satisfied. But when you practice contentment, you can say to yourself, 'Oh yes — I already have everything that I really need.'"

There is a pervasive accumulation-happiness myth. Happiness comes not from what we possess, but from doing something we love, being of service, being connected to a deeper and higher part of us, and being connected to others as in a community which is bound by something common.

The rates of suicide, depression, and loneliness are significantly higher in developed countries versus the developing ones. In most developing countries, extended families have little wealth (thus their money goes to essentials), but they still live together and there are rituals and ceremonies which bind together those in the larger community. Out of necessity, they have learned to be of service and help each other.

Benjamin Franklin told us, "He that is of the opinion money will do everything may well be suspected of doing everything for money." Placing money as our god above everything else engenders fear as we have moved away from our true self. It can also lead to a lowering of integrity as we consider any means to reach our goals.

This accumulation-happiness myth, which many of us hold strongly regarding the economy, is fed by a false belief that everything should increase without having periods of contraction. We are told we should continually produce more so that we can consume more, and this will make us happy. Professionally and personally, we feel our to-do list is endless and we will never get it done. Our self-worth is tied to constant achievement, and this keeps us in a perpetual state of anxiety and fear when we can't get it all done. We are like the gerbil on the exercise wheel, going on and on without knowing or reaching a destination.

Especially in Western society, this collective belief that everything should continually get bigger and that we should conquer nature comes from a collective hubris that has its roots in theology and the concept of manifest destiny. It also comes from a fear of what can happen when contraction occurs — the wheel slows down and we might fall off. This relates to our unwillingness to be still and look inside ourselves, which we cover in later chapters. But as evidenced in nature, contraction is a normal, healthy, and necessary part of the cycle of life.

What if we changed our definition of success to how kind we are, how much light we put in the world, how emotionally healthy our children are, our overall level of joy, or how fulfilled we are in whatever we do to earn an income? These are internal measures of success that an individual can define and control for themselves to a great extent, as opposed to the external measures that we are told are so important. We would not be in excessive fear if these were our measures of success.

Because we were educated in a school system that instilled in us certain expectations and beliefs, most of us have adopted society's messages about success. We are also inundated from birth with marketing that has taught us to look outside of ourselves for success and happiness. Since everyone else is striving for this, it's natural to believe this herd mentality must be the right way. The false belief we hold is that we are not worthy or a success unless we have achieved all of these things, which leads to fear.

Herd mentality has been greatly fed by the fear used in advertising, as this has become the primary tool for marketing products and services. Fear of falling behind is encapsulated in the saying we are not keeping up with the Joneses. We fear not being happy, fear ill health, fear not getting what we rightly deserve. We also fear we won't belong. These are just a few of the tactics of current-day marketing. One needs only to watch commercials or look at the billboards in any major city to see the state of our society and how fear is utilized.

The term "nonessential" has been used extensively with the coronavirus crisis. How many of these products and services that we use as a society *can* be deemed as essential? Do they solely exist to make money for the company offering them, or do they help the world in some way? What if we took all of these resources, skills, and creativity and applied it to products and services that would benefit everyone? Might each of us be much more joyful if we were applying our gifts in something where they could be used for a much higher purpose?

MAIN TAKEAWAY

The expectations we have placed upon ourselves from living in society are misleading and create a lot of fear within us.

If you are striving for a certain level of wealth or success, what is that level? When does it become enough?

"*I am not interested in power for power's sake, but I'm interested in power that is moral, that is right and that is good.*"

MARTIN LUTHER KING JR.

THREE

POWER

TRUE POWER IS USED FOR THE BENEFIT OF EVERYONE BECAUSE it comes from a unitive perspective and an understanding that we are all in this together. Ego power is fear-based and is used solely to benefit the person or group in power. It arises from a separatist perspective based on domination of others and the hoarding of wealth and resources.

Fear-based ego power rarely serves even the interests of a specific constituency, and certainly not the interests of humanity as a whole. This type of ego power and control is central to our world today and operates through most monetary and political systems such as democracy, fascism, monarchy, capitalism, communism, and socialism, as well as many religions. In theory many of these systems sound ideal, but in practice they are corrupt and controlled by individuals seeking wealth and power. Since our world operates from this type of ego power, it is way out of balance.

When power is misused, there is an imbalance in the relationship between those who have the power and misuse it and those on whom the power is being enforced. The former are operating from fear, while the latter are also in fear because they believe they have no choice or feel that submitting will be the easiest path. Others believe they will be rewarded for fitting in.

For instance, in the workplace many in both small to large companies have a constant underlying fear of getting fired, and some managers or leaders play this to their advantage to get extra work. Many companies run their supplier relationships based on fear. "You cut prices by 10%, or you are out." In public companies, this culture of fear starts from the top with the board of directors and the CEO and it extends to shareholders because we have a dysfunctional and shortsighted system where success is measured almost exclusively by a quarterly financial result.

Many of the tech companies and others, such as early stage companies, breed a different kind of fear. This fear is over not being the best, coupled with fear over falling behind and not achieving what everyone else is achieving. I was on a plane with this young guy who worked with one of the top three tech companies. He said that almost everyone works on the weekends because they see others doing it and fear falling behind.

We all know the extreme divisiveness that we have seen with our current political system. It is an "us and them" versus "we" perspective, which can only breed fear. Regardless of political affiliation, we have given our power away to our elected officials by believing that they have our best interests at heart, and this is usually not the case even though some may have entered politics to help people. Why do we keep electing the same officials who have clearly shown that they are in office to benefit themselves?

When we are in fear, we just want someone like the governing authorities to take it away, and we will do anything, including believing what we are told without questioning it, to make this happen. We agree to certain things we would never have agreed to if we weren't in fear, which is what happened after 9-11 and will likely happen after the coronavirus crisis. Because the information and restrictions gradually ramp up, we are like the frog in the pot who is mesmerized and is boiled alive as the temperature of the water slowly rises.

We have also given our power away in terms of our health. Western medicine is excellent in areas such as broken bones or a tumor that needs to be removed, but it has struggled with more gray areas such as chronic illness, which has seen an exponential rise in the last 30 years. Many have turned to alternative medicine, since they have not received solutions from conventional medicine. The latter trains health professionals in a very narrow niche. Treatment is usually a prescription medication which is targeted to symptom relief and often has multiple side effects. This is fundamentally different from addressing the underlying cause of the illness.

Our health professionals are well intentioned, but they often do not have answers for many of the health challenges we are now facing. I am not advocating going away from conventional medicine by any means and I will use it where I feel it's appropriate. What I am suggesting is taking your power into your own hands by doing your own research. When we are open to receiving information from any source that could help us, the Universe will provide this. This could mean any number of things, but each of us needs to know that we need to be the ones in control.

Personally, I had been very healthy until recently but began noticing that my blood pressure was spiking and I was also having bad headaches in the center of my head. I asked my physician to write an order for an MRI, and this ruled out a tumor, but I was shown that my blood vessels are genetically smaller than normal. I have addressed all of my issues very successfully through a large reduction in sodium, taking certain supplements that help with high blood pressure, and really watching how my thoughts create extra stress. I did not find a health professional, alternative or conventional, that told me to do these things, but I worked this out on my own using intuition, knowledge (like results of the MRI), trying several approaches, and logic.

Unfortunately, what I did is the exception. Not only have many given their power away to health professionals and have automatically followed what they say, but we also have a certain subset of people who welcome the attention that being sick brings them and who have made illness their identity. It is classic victim thinking, which is the ultimate way we give our power away. Marketing now plays to this, as if somehow it can be glamorous or cool to be sick. Many want a prescription to solve every health issue because they want a quick fix to these issues.

The health industry is one manifestation of how business and our society has veered off course and how distorted things have become. Health should be based on a proactive versus a reactive model. We all know the horror stories with insurance. When we live in a world where decisions are totally illogical and based on profit, and where others have control of something as critical as our health, there is no way we will escape fear.

Religion is another area that has demonstrated abuse of power, but in most cases each religion was founded by someone who received direct revelation from God. They would never have intended for a man-created structure with rules and dogmas to be added to the simplicity of their teachings. At a minimum, each religion says there is *some thing*, some prayer or rule or type of meditation or spiritual practice we have to do, or that we have go through the priestly class, to reach God. Going further, Western religion has falsely taught that we have done something wrong, that we have "sinned," and that we must do a penance to atone for this. Of course, there is absolutely no way not to live in fear if we believe these things.

All of this is false and an abuse of power that has put a veil over the truth and the knowledge of who we really are. Jesus told us that we are sons and daughters of God like him, that we would do greater things than him, and that we should worship God, not him.

The Bible was edited 300 years after the death of Jesus by men with egos who strived to establish a system of power and control. They decided what writings would comprise the Bible, and they left out certain ones on purpose. Which ones were left out? The ones which further reinforced each of us being divine, in communion with God, a son or daughter of God just as Jesus was. Understanding this would give us power and make their roles unnecessary.

Our fear and rigid beliefs stop us from considering new information that could dramatically alter how we see ourselves and

God. For instance, Jesus spoke Aramaic, and the meanings of words in Aramaic are far different than what was translated into Greek and eventually into English. "Sin" originally meant "error" in Aramaic, while "repent" was "turn the other way." "Turn the other way from your errors" has a completely different tone and meaning from "repent of your sins," but this information is not widely available.

Religion, fear, and God are closely intertwined, and we don't understand how powerful an effect this has on us, especially in the Western world, even if we don't practice religion, any type of spirituality, or even believe in God. Regardless of how loving we understand God to be conceptually, if we hold any shred of belief that we were born in sin and that God will judge and punish us, we will fear God in general and especially what will happen at death. This is the case whether we are a religious fundamentalist, a highly spiritual person, and even for those who profess no belief in a God or a higher power, because it is ingrained in the collective of which we are all a part.

We give our power away because we are in victim mentality and we want the governing authorities, corporations, religious authorities, or the medical establishment to take care of all of our needs and tell us what to do in order to fix our problems. This leads to abuses of power because these authorities are only too willing to take our power if we hand it to them.

We also give our power away to individuals or groups that we are a part of. This can include a spouse, a boss, or a group that influences our beliefs. We give our power to them because we want their approval or because we fear them, as in an abusive situation. However, being disempowered leads to more fear. No one can have power over us unless we *give them* power over us.

It is helpful to understand why others abuse power. This enables us to stay in open-hearted compassion, which keeps us out of fear. Carl Jung said, "Where love rules, there is no will to power; and where power predominates, there love is lacking. The one is the shadow of the other."

MAIN TAKEAWAY

No one has power over us unless we give them that power. Being disempowered can only lead to fear.

 Do you give your power away by assuming someone or some authority knows more than you and will take care of you?

*"If you want to find the
secrets of the Universe,
think in terms of
energy, frequency,
and vibration."*

NIKOLA TESLA

FOUR

ENERGETICS
AND UNITY

———

S O I KNOW WHAT YOU MAY BE THINKING. YOU SEE THIS CHAPTER
title and the above quote, and you are asking why in the world I
am talking about quantum physics if this is a book on releasing fear.
Good question!

The reason I have a chapter on science early on is that in order
to become more self-aware, we have to strip away what we believe to
be false about ourselves and the world around us, which will allow
what's true to be revealed. In this chapter and subsequent ones,
we drill down to the laws and truths at the most basic levels of the
Universe, as they are collectively applicable. We then follow this
with what has shaped each of us individually. The hope is that this
accelerates the questioning process within us and a willingness to
examine and release anything that does not take us towards our goal
of being more joyful and consequently less fearful.

Quantum physics has shown us that everything is in vibration and that frequency is the foundation of life. So each of our cells, everything in the natural world, Earth itself, and even "inanimate" objects carry their own electromagnetic signature. We are electromagnetic beings, which is how tests like EEGs and EKGs work.

Energetics are foundational to the manifest world we see, and only one unified field of energy exists with everything vibrating at different levels. *There is nothing separate, regardless of appearances.*

Even though we don't "see" it because we are seeing through a lens of ego vision, energetics is how everything operates at the most foundational level and affects us in all ways. All of our relationships have their own unique energetics. Certain neighborhoods or cities may feel bad to us, or we may prefer to live on a large plot of land versus high-density housing. A business has its own energetic.

Each of our emotions carries an energetic, and when we describe someone as having bad energy, we are being literal. This is why spiritual teachers talk about raising our vibration. Negativity, anger, resentment, bitterness, unwillingness to forgive, fear — these are all lower vibration emotions that don't feel good. Love, compassion, joy, gratitude — these are higher vibration emotions that make us feel good, and we want more of them.

The system is rigged in our favor as it directs us to what makes us feel good, such as love and joy. Unfortunately, some people want more of the negative and choose to act like a victim, as they erroneously believe this brings them attention in a positive way. The Universe is agnostic on this. It will bring us what we ask for and what we energize, even if we don't know we are asking for it because it comes from a deeply buried belief. This is Universal law 101.

Everyone actually understands energetics. Or, rather, they *feel* the energetics. Some trust this to make decisions much more than others. For instance, we may be talking to someone and they are saying all the right words, but we don't like them for some reason. Something feels off. Trust that. In this case, energetics are much more powerful than how they are trying to deceive us at a surface level by using words. As the coronavirus spread, and stringent measures were being taken in the US, I had conversations with people who I knew were in fear, even though they were saying things completely counter to this. They said that the virus wasn't real or that precautions were not necessary, but I could feel their fear at an energetic level.

When we are in any type of setting, whether this be our relationships, workplaces, or communities, we have to be aware of the energetics of ourselves and others involved. The reason for difficulties or failures goes back to energetics and what is happening at a level beyond appearances or what someone tells us.

We have to be aware of how energetics affect decisions in every area of our lives. For instance, we usually elect politicians, not because they are well qualified (often they are not), but because they are powerful speakers and they draw us in energetically and tell us what we want to hear and what we want to reinforce at the level of our beliefs, even if it's not the best thing for us and others. This can work for the betterment of humanity or the opposite, as in the case of a Hitler.

When we want energetics to flow well, we have to simplify processes. Look at how complicated we have become on the number of societal regulations, tax forms, or getting reimbursed for health procedures with numerous forms and middlemen. This is similar to bad gasoline or old oil in a car that is causing it to stall. Can we mark the physical and energetic decline of a civilization or country by the volume of laws and regulations it has implemented?

Thought is just energy formed into a certain pattern. If that thought is energized enough, it manifests as "reality" in the world we live in. Most people do not realize that their thought, as it manifests individually and collectively, is this powerful and that they need to be very careful what they energize — what they continue to think about and focus on. This is why continual thoughts of fear can be detrimental, as we are literally creating what *could* happen.

Fear is just an energy within us, thus it is not "good" or "bad." As with all energy, it can be transformed and transmuted into something powerful for our benefit and that of the world. How it "works" for us depends on the prism through which we understand and interact with this energy.

In his book *The Holographic Universe*, which I highly recommend, Michael Talbot frequently refers to the work of David Bohm, who was one of the preeminent quantum physicists of the 20th century. Many quantum physicists believe that the Universe is a hologram. In a hologram, each part contains the whole. This aligns with the spiritual traditions that talk about the whole Universe and God being in everything, even just a grain of sand.

Our beliefs are energized thoughts. If they are fixed and not open to change, as is often the case with many of us who experienced traumatic childhoods, we are seeing through a narrow lens and viewing just a small slice of the hologram. We mistake this for reality, when reality is the whole hologram, which is far more encompassing and inclusive than we are seeing. If we can release our conditioning, we are much more capable of seeing reality and not living in fear. For instance, Jesus and others who have performed miracles saw a much broader vision of the whole hologram because they were not limited by a narrow set of beliefs, and this allowed them to work with the laws of the Universe to create miracles.

Science has also shown us that this infinite field of energy in which we exist is relational. For instance, nature has a highly specialized and intelligent way of communicating, like trees on one side of a forest warning trees on the other side about disease. There is an ordered and aware consciousness that underlies all existence, connecting everyone and everything. Like a ripple that is created when you throw a stone into a pond, everything you think, say, and do affects the whole.

So with energetics, science has finally proven what many religious mystics and spiritual traditions have told us. When we say God is One, it does not solely mean that there is one God, although that is certainly true. It means that God is all there exists, and we are part of this oneness. But we see through a narrow, individualized ego lens that makes us believe otherwise. This is the foundational issue where fear is concerned.

MAIN TAKEAWAY

If we understand energetics, we understand how everything works behind appearances and we will see from a much broader perspective that will eliminate fear and allow our life to run smoother.

Where are energetics "off" in your relationships and communities, and how can you change this?

"*Do not dwell in the past; do not dream of the future; concentrate the mind on the present moment.*"

BUDDHA

FIVE

CENTERING
IN THE MOMENT
AND THE HEART

A COROLLARY DISCOVERY BY QUANTUM PHYSICISTS TO WHAT WE discussed in the previous chapter, confirmed in all spiritual traditions, is that space and time do not exist, at least not in the way that we experience them here on Earth. Time is not linear. Everything is happening in the present moment, and it is only our memories (past) and our expectations (future), which are constructs of an ego mind, that lead us to believe in this illusion. In his theory of special relativity, Albert Einstein showed us that time is different according to how fast something is traveling, and this theory has now been confirmed by technology.

This is demonstrated by the twin paradox in physics. One twin blasts off in a spaceship to the nearest star at close to the speed of light while the other twin remains on Earth. After a journey of almost four and a half light years, the spaceship reaches the star and immediately turns around, headed back to Earth. When it reaches Earth, the twin in the spaceship is several years younger based on clocks on Earth and in the spaceship. But the twin in the spaceship doesn't recognize this as both twins are living in the moment, which is all that exists. As Einstein said, "The distinction between the past, present, and future is only a stubbornly persistent illusion."

Life always unfolds in the now. Fear however is always about something in the past or something you expect to happen in the future. Those of us with strong logical minds, a group of which I am a part, are blessed to have this tool. But it can work against us as our mind can create numerous "could happen" and "might be" scenarios which create a lot of fear as our thoughts go down a not-so-good trail. *Why do we place credence in these thoughts when our imagined scenarios rarely happen as we think they will?*

If we can pull our attention back to the present moment, the fear subsides, since this is our natural state. Best-selling author and Buddhist monk Thich Nhat Hanh says, "Fear keeps us focused on the past or worried about the future. If we can acknowledge our fear, we can realize that right now we are okay. Right now, today, we are still alive, and our bodies are working marvelously. Our eyes can still see the beautiful sky. Our ears can still hear the voices of our loved ones."

We have all experienced beautiful moments where we lose track of where we are at, what day of the week it is, and what we are doing, and then our mind stills. Athletes call this "the zone." The problem is that most people don't trust that these glimpses are real as they happen so infrequently, or we believe that we have to do something extraordinary like climb a mountain to experience them. But we can access this state frequently, and we want to allow ourselves to visit as often as possible. This reinforces our true nature, where fear cannot survive. We don't have to do anything to get there except release what's preventing us from seeing that it's our natural state.

Are you making decisions of any kind? This is a rhetorical question to maybe help you realize *how often* you are making decisions. It is actually every moment as there is not a time when we are not choosing something.

In addition to actions and words, we are always choosing what thoughts we want to energize. Random thoughts come in, but then we attach to them and take them one direction or another, or we will choose to let them go and not attach to them. Either way, we are energizing one direction or another. Even when we sleep, there is a higher part of us making decisions.

Witnessing our thoughts is a recommended spiritual practice, one commonly referred to as mindfulness. Watch how we have a thought and it leads to another thought, then another and another, until we have a whole trail of thoughts. When we observe these thoughts, we may first see how meaningless they can sometimes be, but we will definitely notice that these thoughts are always about something in the past or something we think will happen in the future.

They are never in the present moment because that comes from a completely different place within us, one where fear isn't present but one of deep inner wisdom that we want to access for all of our decisions. This is where we can access our higher, divine self. St. Augustine said,

"His knowledge is not like ours, which has three tenses: present, past, and future. God's knowledge has no change or variation."

How do we center ourselves in the now? There is a tremendous amount of powerful writing on how to bring ourselves back to center, so I will not get into a lot here. The essence is found in witnessing and being fully present in what we are doing or saying in each moment. We are witnessing ourselves feeling the razor slide over every inch of our skin, feeling each raindrop splatter on our head, witnessing ourselves having a conversation, witnessing our anger (no better way to defuse the anger), being present with the sharp pain that comes from our chronic illness, or witnessing our breath.

Centering ourselves in the moment requires commitment and practice, because we are so accustomed to living in the ego's thinking mind, which is always either in the past or in the future.

In addition to witnessing, we can center ourselves through practices such as meditation, any creative endeavor such as painting, dancing, or yoga, and especially being in nature. Being grateful is powerful for centering us in the now.

Centering in the now also places us in the heart, for this is the seat of our consciousness. The electromagnetic field coming from the heart is *60 times* larger than the one coming from the brain. Jesus confirmed this in spiritual language: "For where your treasure is, there your heart will be also." Carl Jung, who established analytical psychology, added, "Your vision will become clear only when you can look into your own heart. Who looks outside, dreams; who looks inside, awakens."

Fear contracts and closes our heart space, but we each respond to being fearful in different ways. Many take no action as this is believed to be the safest choice, even though no choice *is* a choice. Helen Keller said, "Avoiding danger is no safer in the long run than outright exposure. The fearful are caught as often as the bold." Ralph Waldo Emerson told us that "Fear defeats more people than any other thing in the world."

A different kind of fear emerged with the coronavirus, as it came up quickly and we held it as one collective, but we each responded in different ways. Many became paralyzed or went into denial, minimizing the seriousness of it, as if it would somehow go away if they didn't acknowledge it. My wife was initially like this when awareness of the virus became widespread.

I was the opposite. I wanted to take whatever action was needed to remedy the fear. It was prudent for us and for our four children, who were spread in different locations, to stock some supplies. As the virus progressed, we had to think through who we needed to bring home, especially the one in NYC who could work remotely and the one still in college who wanted to stay on campus even though the school was strongly recommending against this. We also had to convince them of the seriousness of the situation without them going into a panic, so it became a fine line with numerous people's fears interacting. I wasn't able to be at peace until I had everyone safe and stocked, which I think is what every parent wants.

Until my wife really understood the seriousness of the situation, it didn't work out well as I wanted to take action immediately. I had to act independently, even though she was resisting some of my actions and saying that no one else was reacting this way. My advantage is that as a person with a strong mind, I kicked into some type of logic-based survival instinct that was to our advantage. The downside of this was that I was out of my heart and fear was making me short in my reactions, words, compassion, and patience with my wife and others.

Fear-based thinking is survival-based thinking, and it is rarely logical. Even for those who take action, they are often thinking irrationally. This is why toilet paper is the first thing purchased and hoarded. Fear-based action is never in our best interest.

In his wisdom Confucius told us, "If you look into your own heart, and you find nothing wrong there, what is there to worry about? What is there to fear?" Many of us fear being in our heart because at the core we don't feel we are a good person. In addition to telling us to be in our hearts, Jesus also told us that God is Love. Love is the opposite of fear and is both an emotion and who we are in the fabric of our being. We are one with God and share those attributes. Fred (Mister) Rogers said, "Love isn't a perfect state of caring. It's an active noun, like 'struggle.'" Because we are love, it takes a lot of effort to live in hatred, judgment, and fear, but unfortunately this is what has become habitual for so many, like a rut in the road we can't get our car out of.

Gratitude is also key for centering us in our heart. Centering ourselves in the heart, and therefore the now, has a way of dissolving all of our problems — or at least helping us see them in a different light. The more we practice this, simply through awareness of it happening, the more it will happen. We are only reinforcing what is already there versus reinforcing something false — as the vast majority do almost every moment.

Our education system is strongly geared towards enhancing the mind when it could be balanced with understanding and accessing the wisdom of the heart. Book learning puts us more into our head, which automatically takes us out of our heart and opens the door for fear to enter. Which part of us are we feeding? The more we rely on our thinking mind, the stronger and more entrenched it becomes.

Many of us with advanced degrees are linear thinkers and like to stay in a box or a prescribed set of parameters with which we are comfortable. Then there are some beautifully heart-centered and wise people with only high school degrees. Maybe we need to redefine our definition of wisdom and intelligence.

There is a perfect middle ground. We want to come from our heart while using the mind as a tool. A strong mind used in the right way can be a powerful complement to the heart. But the logical mind should not be in charge. It should be like a hammer we pick up when we need it and then put back down.

Relying on my logical mind was my experience. Because of sexual abuse in my childhood, which created a lot of fear that I carried well into adulthood, I was strongly centered in my thoughts. This was how I believed I could protect myself and stay safe, but this kept me in the cycle of fear. I was never able to understand or feel what was working at an energetic level. I have worked hard to move from my head into my heart and emotions, which has released fear.

If you recognize that you are in your logical mind all the time, there are ways to begin accessing your heart wisdom. The HeartMath Institute (among others) has some simple exercises to help you do this.

"Study the science of art. Study the art of science. Develop your senses — especially learn how to see. Realize that everything connects with everything else." Leonardo da Vinci wasn't talking about seeing through our physical eyes, but about seeing with our heart, our instinct, our compassion, and our innate wisdom.

When we center in the heart and the now, it gives us the opportunity to make incredibly healing choices as we are not reacting unconsciously from fear anymore. We can choose love over fear, compassion over judgment, forgiveness over hatred, and grace over condemnation. *All of our decisions will be exponentially more effective* and right for us and everyone involved.

As you sit here reading this book and are focused on it and nothing else, everything is in perfect order. Only when you allow your thoughts to go to "How am I going to pay this bill?", "How am I going to get that promotion?" (both in the future), or "Why did I say that yesterday?" (in the past) does fear arise and do problems appear. You can literally create an infinite number of problems, but in this moment, you are perfectly okay. For example, you can be grateful you are breathing or that you can see the words in this book.

MAIN TAKEAWAY

The now is all that exists and time and space are only constructs of this three-dimensional world. When we center in this and the heart, we can make conscious choices that are not fear-based.

Very slowly look at what is around you, the contours of your hand, and so forth. Be present to how you turn your head when you do these things. Witness yourself taking these actions.

> *"Nothing can harm you as much as your own thoughts unguarded."*
>
> BUDDHA

WHAT WE SET OUR INTENTIONS TO, WE CREATE

D O YOU FEEL THAT YOUR CURRENT VOCATION AND LIFE situation in general is where you have just been randomly placed, or that there was purposeful intention in getting to this place — on your part or the part of someone else or the Universe?

There is purposeful intention for where we are at, but many do not realize this and thus operate unconsciously, getting caught up in the herd mentality. We can believe it's all random, but the results are not. It's much better to make our intention conscious so we can use it for our benefit as well as that of humanity.

Our beliefs and thoughts (again, these are the same, as our thoughts arise from our beliefs) constitute *our* reality. We will create and manifest something to the extent we feel we are worthy of it *and* to the extent we believe it's possible to create. Jesus multiplied the fish and the bread because he believed anything was possible. Our beliefs can either serve as our jail cell or they can help us soar like eagles.

That's why it is critical to know what our beliefs are and where our blocks to abundance and self-worth lie, especially because these share a bed with our fears, even though most are not aware of this. I dealt with severe self-judgment, which was primarily a result of my sexual abuse (along with shame, guilt, and fear), but I did not understand this or know it was self-judgment until I was in my 30s.

We may want a certain outcome to happen, such as being promoted at our job. But if a subconscious part of us doesn't believe we are worthy of it, energetically we are giving mixed signals to the Universe, and the Universe responds to the direction and how much gas we give it. Our beliefs are our energetics, and we need to be open to them changing as we receive new information.

As mentioned in the last chapter, fear arises from thinking what *could happen*. Usually some kind of outer information triggers this whole trail of meaningless thought that has a negative outcome. But it's very unlikely things will happen in the way we think they will, *unless* we continue to energize that scenario and then actually create it, individually and collectively.

Mother Teresa said, "I will never attend an anti-war rally. If you have a peace rally, invite me." Hopefully, our intention is to bring unity and create healing in our relationships, our workplaces and communities, and in the world. As Mother Teresa was teaching us, be *for* something instead of *against* something. For instance, be *for* eating healthy food versus *against* junk food. The world is in its current situation because we are all against different things, which reinforces the belief in separation, makes us fearful, and makes us see certain individuals, groups, or nations as enemies instead of as our brothers and sisters.

We create using expectation (intention) and gratitude. Once we feel that we are worthy, we expect that something will happen and we are grateful for it *as if* it has already happened. This is how Jesus performed miracles. Any outcome is possible. We are only limited by *what we think is not possible.* When we are in fear, there is a lot we think is not possible. Fear makes us react from a place of seeing limited options for resolving a problem, while making the problem appear much worse.

When we expect something amazing to happen and we are grateful for it happening, even though it has not yet happened, we are laying the most important foundation for the house we are building. It is the same as planting seeds in a garden and knowing they will sprout even though we can't see them. Energetics is what is happening to the seed under the ground. We have to water the seed with continued intention and faith that it will sprout and with the feeling of joy for what it will become.

We always can choose love over fear (there is an amazing song by a friend of mine, Shawn Gallaway, called "I Choose Love"). All we need to do is set our intention and will to choose it, and then do it. Even if we don't get it right to start, it will bring great awareness to us and we will increasingly move into love the more we practice it.

MAIN TAKEAWAY

What we think is very powerful and creates what happens in our life. This can be fear-based or unity-based.

 Where have you focused your intentions? Do you feel this has been positive or negative for you?

"Nothing ever exists entirely alone; everything is in relation to everything else."

BUDDHA

SEVEN

EVERYTHING IS A VEHICLE AND IS RELATIONAL

A S WE COME TO A GREATER UNDERSTANDING ON HOW THE Universe works and our role in it, we begin to see patterns of how everything fits together like a puzzle and how the Universe is helping us. We come to realize that everything serves as a means to an end, and as a vehicle to show us what we have falsely believed so that we may release it and come to a greater understanding that we are not the victim of our circumstances.

We are the creators of our circumstances via our will, attitude, and as mentioned in the last chapter, our intention. Once we understand this, we can discover our true gifts and use them to help the world as well as live in full joy. The Universe will open many doors for us to do that, which will strengthen our faith, a topic we will explore in a later chapter.

Nothing is random in the Universe. You can't have some things that have meaning while others do not. That would be like someone being partially pregnant. "Random" things do happen to us because we are part of a whole and we are subject to the actions of others, but whatever action the other person, group, or governing authority took was not random because they chose that action. And we *choose how we want to react* to their action, which is true power.

Now we begin to understand that we are much more than the role we play and we are here for a greater purpose of learning, remembrance, and helping others and the world. Our identity is not what we do, nor how we are seen by others. We are not the high-powered businessman or the esteemed doctor, not the star athlete, not the well-known researcher or theologian, not the member of a prominent family or the member of a rejected or oppressed class of society, not the middle child or the forgotten grandmother. These are just roles that serve as vehicles used by the Universe to facilitate our learning and remembrance.

Just as if we are an actor in a play, we play the role to the best of our ability, but we can do this in full awareness that it is a role. This makes it fun and makes it so that we don't fall into fear or judgment.

Unfortunately, most people, especially if they are in careers which are highly praised by the world, get caught up in their roles and think this is their true identity. They love the adulation or notoriety, and they don't want to give this up. This often stems from self-worth issues. But it's the ego that loves this while our higher selves know this is false. Our task is to allow our higher self to come more to the forefront, as the vast majority of people experience life only through an ego lens, which can be tiring and scary. A Chinese proverb says, "Tension is who you think you should be. Relaxation is who you are." We must take our power back from these false identities through which we have viewed ourselves.

The vehicles that the Universe uses to help us become more self-aware are really everything in life, not just our roles. They are our dreams, the book that happened to be left on the chair at the doctor's office, how our heart sings when we think about our loved ones, how we feel when our supervisor yells at us without a good reason, the deep sadness when someone passes, the awe of the Grand Canyon or a beautiful cloud formation, the hawk that flies right above our windshield, and especially our direct relationships with ourselves, with others, and with the organizations and communities of which we are a part.

The Universe is constantly talking to us and giving us hints if we will just pay attention. It sets us up, but always in a loving way that's for our highest good. It creates the perfect school for us to learn and remember.

Some vehicles serve us both individually and collectively. Depending on how it's used, a vehicle can take us away from recognition of our unity instead of towards it.

Sports is a good example of this. Sports is huge in our culture and has a bipolar effect on society. I was a player, a coach of many recreational teams, and a too-attached parent involved with numerous travel teams. I needed my child to do well for my feelings of self-worth. As a fan of both college and pro sports teams, I hated the competing fan base.

The benefits of sports are numerous, especially the unitive aspect of bonding on a team. However, the positive effects of what sports are meant to do for us are overshadowed by what they have become. Divisiveness and an "us versus them" mentality pervade rabid fan bases, and even owners and university administrators. Some coaches cheat or abuse their athletes to win at all costs. Sports is a business where profitability and power rule, and integrity is often tossed out the door.

We have become so distorted in our obsession around sports and celebrities that we pay someone who can throw a football, dribble a basketball, or act in a movie millions of dollars and put them on a pedestal, giving them our power and expecting them to have great wisdom when they are simply human like everyone else.

Sports no longer provides a proper model of competitiveness and playing just for sheer joy without regard for the results. Being competitive served us well when we were cavemen and had to worry about where our next meal was coming from, but it doesn't serve us well in terms of understanding who we are as one humanity. I used to be highly competitive in sports, card games, and board games. I was proud of my abilities. Now I am happy if others win so that they can feel good about themselves, and I am grateful for this change in myself. Seeing from a unity perspective means we build each other up, not tear each other down and try to beat the hell out of the competition.

I have recognized many significant vehicles for healing in my life, especially in my close relationships and in the business world where I have had a wide amount of experience. I am a member of an entrepreneurial Jewish family that has founded and built a number of businesses from a large office supply wholesaler to a mid-sized family printing business, which I currently work for. I have also either worked for or been involved with many Fortune 100 corporations, and I have had early-stage entry and investment into two startups which failed, and a third one I cofounded, HUSO sound therapy, which has been successful.

HUSO was one of the major vehicles in my life as it made me face my belief that tied money to self-worth, which was inherited from society and from my family over many generations. It is a belief that a majority of people in the western world hold. HUSO is both a software and hardware business that required a significant amount of capital, and it was initially funded solely with personal resources. As our personal funds dwindled and we had to take out an additional mortgage to fund a line of credit, this created a lot of fear in me. The only way through the fear was to heal the false beliefs that were propping it up.

Unfortunately, many of us resist our vehicles and we are unwilling to look at what the Universe is trying to show us. We can't move to the next learning opportunity until we pass the one we are on. Everyone knows of others who continually encounter the same difficult circumstances or who repeat the same mistakes in business or in their personal relationships.

For instance, a person might have moved from company to company and had three managers in a row that were condescending. Or they have had repeated personal relationships with someone who was emotionally shut down or condescending. Again, this is not random. This is the Universe bringing up a self-worth issue. Many won't take responsibility and they try to blame something outside of themselves like their job, manager, or the person they are in the relationship with, but it's never about the other person and what they say or do. The person with whom we are angry is just giving us a mirror to help us see what we believe is lacking within us or what we don't like about ourselves. They are giving us a *gift*, but often it doesn't feel that way and resistance arises in us.

As briefly discussed earlier, science has shown that the Universe is relational. Nothing exists on its own but exists only in relationship to something else. So our vehicles for growth are all relational. We are in a relationship with every individual in our life, even those we encounter only briefly. We are in a type of relationship with our workplaces and communities. We are in relationship to Earth and nature. We are in a relationship with ourselves, and we can only be aware of this by looking inside. And we are in a relationship with whatever we define as a higher power.

Quantum physicist David Bohm said, "The essential feature in quantum interconnectedness is that the whole universe is enfolded in everything, and that each thing is enfolded in the whole." As we are in our individual relationships, we are also in relationship to the whole. If we don't recognize the interconnectedness of everything, fear will result.

MAIN TAKEAWAY

Nothing exists on its own. Everything has meaning only in relation to something else. Because of this, everything serves as a vehicle to help us recognize we are not our roles and we are here to learn and remember.

 What do you recognize as the most significant vehicle in your life and what has it taught you? What is the current vehicle in your life that is causing you the most angst, and what beliefs is it triggering that you are resisting?

"Truth is the property of no individual but is the treasure of all men."

RALPH WALDO EMERSON

EIGHT

TRUTH

———

WE HAVE BEEN DISCUSSING WHAT WE CAN CALL UNIVERSAL Laws, and in this chapter we are going to stay with that general theme but come from a little different angle. It is the confusion over what truth is that creates fear and anxiety for so many.

A large majority of people believe that certain individuals and groups are "right" on an issue and have the truth, while others are "wrong." Of course, each individual believes that they fall into the group that has the truth. Sometimes this is taken further with the belief that those who are "wrong" are "bad people" who should be condemned and vilified. Albert Einstein said, "Whoever undertakes to set himself up as a judge of Truth and Knowledge is shipwrecked by the laughter of the gods."

There is an Absolute Truth that is the very foundation of existence, and there is also a personal reality or relative truth we each hold, hopefully one that comes from being in balance and living as an open and authentic human being. Absolute Truth and our relative truth coexist within us.

Absolute Truth is not what we each choose it to be. It is *what it is*. Gandhi stated this well: "Truth is by nature self-evident. As soon as you remove the cobwebs of ignorance that surround it, it shines clear." There is only one Absolute Truth which we share and which we are. Your power comes from living in Absolute Truth.

Absolute Truth is not something which can be "spun" or is up for debate, for then it cannot be Truth. It's not beliefs or opinions or what someone else has told us, since these all change. Absolute Truth has no opposite and is changeless.

Then there is a personal truth which is how we see things and is our interpretation of reality. This is what is "right" and "wrong" for each of us, and this is a "truth" that will change as we grow in awareness and perspective.

Look at how our beliefs change, sometimes even in a short period when new info has been revealed. Based on this, why would we ever place any credence in our current beliefs and hold on to them as if our life was dependent on it? We *think* our life is dependent on it, but that is just a belief! So it's very helpful if we understand our version of reality to be just our version.

It's best to live our relative or personal truth from a balanced perspective. We carefully examine the evidence, without our previous biases playing into it, and we determine what rings true for us. We also understand that someone else's personal truth is different and we respect this. No one holds the same set of beliefs, and everyone acts based on those beliefs they regard as truth. Someone may think that something is true, but it is really their truth. If we had their exact set of experiences, like a certain kind of trauma in their life, we might hold the same personal truth and beliefs they do.

Knowing that everyone has their own truth and acts from this, how can we truly judge anyone else? The above is critical for anyone to be a compassionate human being and an effective and respected leader in any type of organizational or community setting.

Because relative or personal truth is being mistaken for Absolute Truth, a balanced perspective is not how most people see the many controversial issues that are currently creating major divisiveness in our society. Those at the far ends of the political, religious, and other spectrums are not willing to take a look at their beliefs, biases, and motives. Either they don't see them because they have become completely blinded by fear, or they see them but just don't care because they may place something like accumulation of power or wealth, or unwillingness to face their beliefs, above anything else, which is also fear.

As Danish philosopher Søren Kierkegaard told us, "There are two ways to be fooled. One is to believe what isn't true; the other is to refuse to believe what is true." When we have become completely hardened in our beliefs and won't allow any logic or reason to be considered, even when we are presented with evidence that is irrefutable, nothing can be resolved as everything is viewed as "us versus them" as opposed to the unitive "we," and this is all from fear. This has been the state of our society.

Many of the controversial issues have a middle ground that is in balance and makes logical sense if the parties discussing it were open to releasing their biases and putting themselves in the other person's shoes. For instance, vaccines are highly controversial. It is clear from many years of history and the eradication of certain diseases that vaccines have saved many lives and have benefited humanity. On the other hand, a large number of mothers and pediatricians have reported children having severe reactions and major long-term health consequences from vaccines. Finally, it is clear that there is a large vested money interest in vaccines and an increasing number of them have been pushed in the last 30 years.

The collective personal truth is that all of these realities exist simultaneously. If we lived in a normal world and this issue could be looked at from a balanced and rational perspective, and especially a unitive one where everyone was looking out for each other, the parties would be able to get together and discuss the best path forward that serves everyone, which might include determining which children were more likely to have a reaction because of genetics or because the mother had been exposed to something environmentally when pregnant. Then an alternative course of action for these more susceptible children could be determined.

We don't live in a normal world. Everyone has their vested interest *and few are looking out for each other as part of one humanity.* We can't change the health consequences of what has happened to these children, but we can honor them and their pain through balancing what has transpired. We do this by acknowledging responsibility and by choosing to do things differently going forward.

There is a lot we are not being told by many sources from individuals to corporations to governing authorities. Keeping secrets engenders fear, because we can feel energetically that something is being withheld from us.

But we hold equal responsibility to those withholding information, since we are like children as most of us have not done work on ourselves where we can take in information and process it without panicking. We live in a fantasy reality, which is great for a child, but not for an adult. Thus as we discussed earlier in the book, someone or something outside of us makes the decision for us as to what we can handle. They take our power by filling an energetic vacuum that was created through not knowing ourselves and our power at the deepest levels.

Living both in Truth and what I call a pure version of my truth have been extremely important to me, and sometimes I have been self-judgmental to a large degree when I have failed to live up to my own expectations and standards. This search for Truth has driven my willingness to look at anything that has not served me and release it. For me, it is kind of like a poison I want out of my body. Thus, although I will often initially become defensive, I take in what those who love me say about me and see if it's true. If it is, I will ask the Universe and God for help in changing it as quickly as possible (and I have had to learn great patience when it comes to timing).

Being willing to look at our beliefs and change them is the key to a cessation of fear and becoming a self-aware individual who can truly help the world. Philosopher René Descartes told us very directly what we need to do when he said, "If you would be a real seeker after truth, it is necessary that at least once in your life you doubt, as far as possible, all things."

Absolute Truth along with an open and unbiased personal truth is something well worth striving for as there are many positive offshoots of this besides cessation of fear, such as kindness and fulfillment. Writer Khalil Gibran says, "Truth is a deep kindness that teaches us to be content in our everyday life and share with the people the same happiness."

Being in Truth leads to humility. "True knowledge exists in knowing that you know nothing." Socrates is telling us that we don't know all that we *think* we know. This leads us to humility and the ability to truly serve. Paradoxically it allows our higher selves to come to the forefront and give us true knowledge, which we can use highly effectively in all areas of our lives.

If we really aren't certain of anything and if we make no judgments, it is kind of difficult to be fearful as we aren't focused on something specific. We are just going with the flow and fear cannot attach itself to anything.

MAIN TAKEAWAY

Truth is not the entitlement of one individual or group. It is the right and essence of everyone.

What have you been certain is true in the past where you now see it differently? Going forward, are you willing to allow not being so certain about things?

> *"Man's task is to become conscious of the contents that press upward from the unconscious."*

CARL JUNG

NINE

OUR STORY AND PERSONAL CONDITIONING

A S WE INTRODUCED IN EARLIER CHAPTERS, WE ARE EACH A product of collective and societal conditioning, and in this chapter we explore some of the personal conditioning that we each uniquely hold.

Our personal conditioning is both genetic and environmental. As described previously with the mention of intergenerational trauma, we likely inherit certain genetic patterns from our ancestors that they experienced environmentally, such as trauma. As the human race, we all hold similar beliefs in our DNA that manifest as certain present-day fears.

For instance, as hunter-gatherers our ancestors' greatest fear would have been exclusion from the family and the tribe, because this was a certain death sentence. So this may manifest today as fear of missing out and not being part of the crowd, which can be dangerous if something doesn't benefit the "herd" and we are being driven off a cliff. This type of psychology is why people buy on the rebounds and ride a bear market stock decline until they are decimated.

Looking at our personal environmental conditioning, it has been verbal, nonverbal or implicit, and action-based. We grew up with parents or adults, usually well-intentioned but sometimes not, who told us certain things about life, people, a belief or non-belief in a higher power, and how they felt about themselves. This was all told through their biases, prejudices, fears, and history — conditioning or abuse that had been passed on to them. We watched them be workaholics or alcoholics and thought this was normal. We believed everything they told us or showed us, because that is what children do and because children feel this is the only way they can survive. I am reminded of the Harry Chapin song "Cat's In The Cradle" — "I'm gonna be like you, dad. You know I'm gonna be like you."

We learn what our parents expect of us. "You have to be quiet to be good, you have to take care of me, everything is your fault, why can't you be more like your brother, you are only worthy and I only love you if you offer your body to me for my sexual urges, or you will be killed if you try to stop me when I am in a drunken rage." These are the "sins" of the fathers being passed down.

There is an infinite number of ways in which we have been conditioned and believe we need to act in order to survive. Children understand the need to conform to survive, and they are sponges, but what if the sponge is soaking up polluted water? Many adults exist in abusive personal or workplace situations, often repeating what happened in childhood. We may have taken in and believed what a supervisor or a boyfriend said about us that was completely wrong.

Adding in the society conditioning we discussed in the earlier chapter, we have been conditioned from many sources, and this has not served us well. If we deny how this conditioning has affected us, we will be driven by unconscious motives and defenses and especially fear, and we will have dysfunction in all areas of our life. Thus, we must *unlearn* many things we have falsely believed about ourselves. Belief does not make for reality. The philosopher Antisthenes said, "The most useful piece of learning for the uses of life is to unlearn what is untrue."

This colored lens through which each of us sees the world is unique for each person. Hopefully, if we are willing to grow, it changes as we are exposed to new information on a moment-to-moment basis. Think of how our beliefs have evolved over time.

What are the upsides to stepping back from our biases and releasing our conditioning? They are numerous. First, we will be much happier and peaceful as fear comes from a strong attachment to certain beliefs. Second, we will be more open and able to work with Universal flow to bring us what we want. Third, we will discover our unique gifts and how best to utilize them. Finally, within our personal lives, workplaces, and other communities, we will be much more effective with our decision making and relationships because we will see a larger part of the picture instead of just the slice we have been conditioned to see.

MAIN TAKEAWAY

We are the product of our conditioning, and we must release that conditioning so we can be more joyful and make decisions in our lives from a much broader perspective.

Think how you see the world and yourself. Where did this come from? How were you conditioned so that these beliefs were the end result, and do the confines of your colored lens enable you to be who you would like to be?

> "*Knowing yourself is the beginning of all wisdom.*"

ARISTOTLE

TEN

HOW TO RECOGNIZE OUR CONDITIONING AND RELEASE IT

I T SEEMS FAIRLY OBVIOUS, BUT IN ORDER TO MOVE TO A NEW STORY and not live in fear, *we have to want to release our conditioning and the old story.* Unfortunately, there is always resistance to this because our conditioning is what we are accustomed to even though it has been detrimental. At some level we feel that our beliefs keep us safe, especially if they were something that truly did keep us safe in childhood.

Most of us have the same virus, and I am not referring to the coronavirus. It's like a computer virus that runs underneath the surface, one that we don't know is there but that greatly affects the operation of *us*. Like a computer virus, it is in control and it shapes who we are and what we do. It is a message of self-judgment. The message can be "I am not worthy" or "I am not lovable." Or it might be "I have sinned and I should be punished." It can take many forms.

Those who exhibit the strongest egos and the greatest need for control, and those who cast themselves as victims, are the ones who believe in these messages the strongest, but they operate in vastly different ways.

Those with strong egos make sure that they have control in terms of power and money. Those who take the victim tact try and elicit pity, which is a different type of control, in an unsuccessful attempt to bolster their negative internal messaging. Some people do both. But we all have this virus to some extent, and to get what we want, most of us have acted both from a strong ego and as a victim at different times. Some are aware of these patterns and working on them, while others have buried any recognition of them.

Because it's natural to resist pain of any kind, many people stay in what the psychological community calls the "pain body," and this is closely intertwined with our fear. We create all kinds of defenses. Dysfunctional patterns arise as justifications or excuses to avoid facing and healing the pain and looking within. But we can begin the process of releasing our conditioning by watching our reactions as we go through life.

Judgment and projection are two primary defense mechanisms. Carl Jung explained, "Projection is one of the commonest psychic phenomena. Everything that is unconscious in ourselves we discover in our neighbor and we treat him accordingly."

He also said, "Everything that irritates us about others can lead us to an understanding of ourselves." The Universe brings us those people who will act as mirrors for us.

We judge others because they have attributes we do not like in ourselves, or we judge what we see in others and we wish we had in ourselves. Judgment is a projection of self-judgment or it comes from fear. These are basically the same thing because if we are in self-judgment, we are in fear. I could never figure out why I judged others so severely, and this bothered me a great deal, but one day I finally understood that this was my own self-judgment being projected out. Collectively, we see projection to a very heightened degree in the blame that is rampant in our society.

Projection often involves anger, and when anger is present, it's almost always coming from fear. This rarely leads to a good outcome. Buddha said, "In a controversy, the instant we feel anger we have already ceased striving for truth, and have begun striving for ourselves."

Anger is a pointer, and if we want to grow and get out of fear, we need to be willing to see where anger is pointing us. Sometimes we are angry at another person, group, or authority who isn't acting in our best interest or the best interest of the world. Our anger will point us to what is out of balance but also to how we can come from compassion. But as described above, usually our anger is a projection of our beliefs, especially self-judgment, which makes it look like the issue is something eternal to us.

Anger points us to an inner belief system we are bumping up against and we don't want to look at. For instance, we may get angry and defensive if someone accuses us of something, but this happens because we partially believe it's true at some level and we judge ourselves for it, regardless of whether it's true or not. If we don't believe it's true, we just let it go and there is no anger present.

With projection there are often other accompanying negative emotions such as resentment, bitterness, condemnation, or self-pity. If we simply recognize that someone is selfish, this isn't projection. If we get angry about it or want to harshly condemn them, then we are trying to project self-judgment over the belief we are also selfish. We may or may not be selfish, but we believe we are. Projection involves our shadow parts, which we fear to face. Anytime we suppress a part of ourselves, we are creating a perceived schism within ourselves and we have lost our power.

When Jesus told us, "Judge not, that ye be not judged," he was not saying we would be judged by God. He was saying that we are judging ourselves.

How can we change this dynamic? We pull back our blame, judgments, and individual projections and heal ourselves. Again, our relationships, especially our close ones, serve as a mirror to practice this. We often project images of our parents on to our partners in an attempt to heal what we were not given.

The next time we are angry and want to blame someone, can we take a deep breath and not act or speak from this space? We can ask someone to take responsibility for their actions without blaming them. Anger, projection, blame, and fear are four legs of the same stool.

How do we want to interact with the other person? Where is this anger inside of us coming from, and do we realize the other person is just giving us a gift to help us see this? What beliefs do we hold that are making us have this reaction, and what experiences did we have that these beliefs are tied to? It's not what the other person says or does, *it is our reaction* to what they say or do that leads us to a greater understanding of what we need to bring into the light.

It was again Jung, ever the fountain of wisdom on the nature of psychology and conditioning, who said, "There is no birth of consciousness without pain." Instead of resisting the pain, can we embrace it as a necessary part of our growth?

Starting from the time we enter the world, pain is part of the human experience, and a lot of mental and emotional growth comes from surrender and acceptance of things we cannot change, along with the realization that we have immense fortitude. We are much stronger than we think we are. Henry Ford said, "One of the greatest discoveries a man makes, one of his greatest surprises, is to find he can do what he was afraid he couldn't do." This includes facing our perceived inner demons.

I have never liked being in healing periods that involved grief, depression, or anger, but I have always been grateful for the false that was released in me, the joy on the other side, and subsequently the power that I came to know within me.

My sexual abuse by my mother created a lot of fear within me, along with shame, guilt, and highly distorted beliefs around love. Well into my adulthood, I had a lot of anger when there were situations I couldn't control, which was literally my 12-year-old self acting out, as I didn't feel in control at the time of the abuse. I still feel uncomfortable at not having control over an outcome, and sometimes that becomes severe if I feel that someone I love could be in danger by taking some action. Others may not have been overtly abused as I was, but many felt judged and unloved in childhood, and this will manifest in ways such as an inability to be open and vulnerable in relationships and being highly self-judgmental.

When we are in our pain body and with fear in general, most of us try to stuff it or medicate it, sometimes several ways at once — drugs and alcohol, food, porn or affairs, accumulation of wealth, status, and power, excessive technology or social media, or having to be in control. Name anything and there is likely someone using it in a not-so-good way to medicate their fear. I found that I was stuffing my fear around the coronavirus with food and eating when I wasn't even hungry.

The strategy of stuffing or medicating our fear doesn't work. It may seem like it works temporarily, but the fear is still there and then builds even more because it's trying to get our attention. We are very good at fooling ourselves about what we are facing and what we need to address. As Rudyard Kipling clearly stated, "Of all the liars in the world, sometimes the worst are our own fears."

Staying in dysfunction will manifest in every area of our life and do more than rob us of joy and the ability to have authentic relationships. For instance, it has been shown that unresolved and repressed emotions can lead to physical illness, such as repressed anger manifesting in depression or cancer. We are really limiting who we can be when we operate from a false self. Rumi said, "Do not sell yourself at a ridiculous price, you who are so valuable in God's eyes."

The Universe teaches and we learn through contrast. By seeing who we are not — that we are not the roles we play, that we are not this angry, anxious, or depressed person, but only temporarily experiencing these states — we see who we are. By seeing what we do not want and who we do not want to be, we see what we do want and who we do want to be.

The times when I'm not in fear greatly contrast with the times when I am in fear and strongly point out to me how bad fear feels. I will do anything not to be there. This is the power of contrast, which can be a great impetus for change. Many do not experience this contrast around fear as strongly, as they stay in a constant level of underlying fear and they never know the freedom and feeling of not being in fear.

Many choose to continue on the path of "what we don't want and who we are not" behaviors. The Universe will continually try to help us by giving hints if we are not moving in the proper direction, and it will increase the intensity of these reminders if we are not paying attention. We are not being punished. Our higher selves in conjunction with the Universe have chosen healing and remembrance, and we are just being given opportunities to fulfill this.

As we examine our conditioning and work to release it, it is important we ignore society or family conditioning, which is often clothed in "a man should not cry" or "a woman should not get angry." This is taking our power back. But we have to be careful with anger as it can be destructive. It's not okay to direct it at anyone just because we feel it, nor should someone abuse it in the workplace because they have the power to do so. Jesus showed us with the fig tree what happens when anger is unrestricted — he killed it.

When we have trauma that we aren't dealing with, we are always working strategies and defenses to control situations and relationships. This prevents us from having fully authentic and open relationships, as this requires vulnerability and no game-playing. We fear being vulnerable, but it is one of the most powerful things we can do for our fear, as long as the vulnerability doesn't come from victimhood. Vulnerability and openness in our personal and workplace relationships doesn't mean being weak. We can be vulnerable and firm and strong at the same time.

Earlier, we briefly mentioned acting like a victim. When we are healing ourselves or even healing an organization or community that has gone through traumatic times, it's important we acknowledge the trauma we experienced, but not act as a victim. Victimization arises from fear and can show itself in many ways, such as always seeing the negative, wanting attention through pity, or righteous indignation at being falsely judged or misrepresented. It's important for us to recognize that acting like a victim gives our power away. *It is our choice* whether we take offense at someone judging us, whether there is any truth in what they are saying or not. Also, we may think they are judging us when that isn't the case. Our minds can really deceive us, especially when we have hardened belief systems.

I saw myself as a victim intermittently for many years, and I blamed others, often my wife who was an angel to stay with me. I also blamed situations, the Universe, God — whatever fit the bill at that time to be the perfect recipient of my anger. One thing I had to keep reminding myself of was that I could look at my reactions and know that this was about me, not something external to me. I asked what the belief was that was behind my reaction, because awareness of the belief is the first step in releasing it.

We can temporarily be in self-pity but we don't want to stay there as it is really a defense against dealing with an experience or examining a false belief and moving past it. Helen Keller, who could have easily fallen into self-pity, said, "Self-pity is our worst enemy and if we yield to it, we can never do anything wise in this world."

Society and business feed the victim and thus the fear mentality. Look at the marketing messages for the legal industry, especially the injury attorneys. They all boil down to, "You have been victimized and you should be compensated." We are encouraging something which completely goes against who we want to be individually and as a society.

When we reflect on the above statement on self-pity by Helen Keller, who was dealing with significant handicaps, it will hopefully put us in a space of gratitude for all of the blessings in our life. The greatest thing we can do to take us out of our self-pity and victim mentality is to be grateful and to do something for others, especially something that no one else knows about.

When we do something for others, we are also doing it for ourselves as this takes us outside of ourselves and outside of a "poor me" mentality, placing us in a unity perspective. We are also outside of a fear mentality. From this space, healing and growth can occur much more rapidly.

Our growth in self-awareness and removing ourselves from a fear mentality will *create ripples that extend far beyond what we recognize*. Each of us can have that big an impact, because when we do our individual parts, it feeds into the collective and change happens. We have to stop blaming each other out of our fears and come together to solve our problems instead of everyone acting out of self-interest or righteous indignation.

MAIN TAKEAWAY

We become self-aware by witnessing our reactions and tracing them back to the beliefs that have created this reaction. As we do this, we release our conditioning and fear, and we become a powerful carrier of change for the world.

What is one main belief you recognize that is causing you to be in fear? Is this an outer belief that has an underlying one attached to it? How would you like to change this, and how can you accomplish this?

> *"For what shall it profit a man, if he shall gain the whole world, but lose his soul?"*
>
> JESUS

ELEVEN

THE EGO

WE EACH HAVE A CHOICE, AND LET'S BE CLEAR WHAT THAT choice is. Will we set our intention and our personal will to promote unity, healing, and a collective greater good? Or will we set it to benefit ourselves and certain individuals or special interest groups we belong to? Martin Luther King Jr. told us that "Every man must decide whether he will walk in the light of creative altruism or in the darkness of destructive selfishness."

If we choose the ego and self-interest, we are operating from a very limited perspective. It may temporarily *appear* that we have won and that we have accumulated all of this wealth or power and control, but we have really lost. We have lost the opportunity to fulfill the purpose of what our higher self came here to do, because it didn't come here to make a lot of money or to have people put us on a pedestal. These things may be the vehicles through which we learn and remember, but they are only a means to an end.

We have also lost an opportunity to be a light for and in service to others, which is the most powerful and joyous thing we can do. To be a light takes us out of fear. This is one of the main purposes of our experience on Earth, and as we do this, we receive it back one hundred-fold for we are one. We must stand in the power, and especially the responsibility, of who we truly are as part of one whole.

The ego operates through judgment and comparison. For instance, witness our initial thoughts when we meet or see someone for the first time. We usually label them in many ways, making judgments about how they look, how they speak, how they are driving too fast or too slow (we all look over to see who is driving the car). The ego needs to label or categorize everything to feel safe. It compares, and the result is we feel better than the other person or group — we have more money, are better looking, or are smarter than this person. Or we feel worse, telling ourselves, "My body is fat compared to her body." In unity, everything is equal. We appreciate differences *while knowing they are only an appearance.*

If we compare to others, we will be in fear because we can never be satisfied with who we are. One of the most detrimental ways we compare is to our younger selves, especially how our bodies used to be or how our brains functioned better. As we age, this type of comparison plays into several fears, including our fear that we are not good enough as we are and our fear of death.

The ego is always in fear. It needs answers or it will be in a greater fear, so it pushes the mind to come up with a solution. This is one of the reasons we continually stay in our thoughts.

The ego also feeds itself on grievances. It has righteous anger. It wants to stay in resentment, bitterness, anger, judgment, self-pity, and pride. Watch your thoughts, since the ego is always looking for something to judge or worry about.

The ego also loves guilt and fear, and these have become a tenet of Western religion, though they are not of God. The ego uses fear and guilt to try and control situations and achieve its agenda. The ego identifies with the body and sees others only as bodies, not as spirit, which creates the foundation for the illusory belief in separation. This is why people want to keep their bodies looking young and we have a plethora of products, including plastic surgery for literally every body part, to fulfill this unhealthy need. Our task is to look past the body to see the higher self within, as this is what's real.

Our spirit rests in perfect peace and certainty, needing nothing additional. The ego is always looking for the next thing to satisfy it. This is a fruitless search, for there is no goal that satisfies it and we will never find happiness in this way. Thus billionaires want to accumulate more wealth, pro athletes more awards, professionals more recognition, and addicts more drugs. This is one of the reasons few take time to become still and know themselves at a deeper level.

I want to distinguish between the terms happiness and joy as they have been used somewhat interchangeably throughout the book. This is an important distinction as happiness is related to ego desires, which is why it comes and goes. We are happy when the stock market goes up or our team wins, but we are depressed when the stock market goes down or our team loses. We need to get off this rollercoaster as it's not how we are meant to live our lives. Joy on the other hand is intrinsic. We can reach a place where we feel it all the time, even under difficult life circumstances.

Our egos do not control us, nor are they separate from us. They are a byproduct of what is needed to exist in this Earth reality, but they are created from and exist only in judgment. They exist on a foundation of quicksand, which is why they are unstable. Most of us let the ego drive our lives, instead of being guided by the diamond within.

For a long time I thought I had to overcome my ego to reach the spiritual ideals I wanted to operate within, and I judged myself when I didn't feel I was meeting my standards. But it was my ego judging my ego, since our spirit does not judge.

When we let go of the false, our spirit naturally comes to the forefront of our consciousness. Our spirit is eternal and its foundation is a rock. If we feel depressed, anxious, or fearful all the time, it's because we see our identity solely as ego-based, which is a scary and unstable place to be. In that space, we believe everything is separate from us and we truly feel alone. The Dalai Lama elucidated this well: "Too much self-centered attitude, you see, brings, you see, isolation. Result: loneliness, fear, anger. The extreme self-centered attitude is the source of suffering."

When we believe something is separate from us, we fear it and try to control it so we can stay safe. This is collectively playing out in an extreme way in the appearance of the world, which has been descending into chaos and insanity as it comprises many people who are fearful, greedy, and abusive of power.

Business is just the aggregate of all of the individual egos of its employees. As the energetic head of the business, if the CEO is highly ego-centered, then the business will also reflect this as there will be a culture of fear and lack of integrity. It will gather and hoard as much resources as it can and treat employees and suppliers as chattel. If the CEO or owner comes from more of a unity perspective, then the business will reflect this.

Each of us is being asked to reduce the influence of the ego and to see in a one-hearted way. We are being asked to live from an open heart, raising our understanding so that we can fulfill the role we are meant to play in order to help the world. We do this with forgiveness, and we are presented opportunity after opportunity to practice this.

We have to *want* and actively work to reduce the ego's influence by forgiving, apologizing, taking responsibility, admitting we are not right, wanting to be happy instead of right, releasing bitterness and resentment, not speaking when we are angry, and by not blaming and letting our emotions overcome us. This can be hard at times, but we have to summon our will and push through it.

A strong mind is highly praised in Western society and rightfully so, but it has to be balanced with the heart and inner guidance. This is rare. A vast majority of people are making decisions from an unconscious place, which means the decisions are often not aligned with their inner truth and thus are meaningless. The greatest thing we can understand is that we don't understand anything. Recall the quotation by René Descartes. This opens us up to receive higher guidance, as we are now operating from humility. Humility is the ego's opposite.

Don't be afraid of not knowing. We have to first be willing to not know before we can receive guidance. Then we will have all of the answers we need, and they will be for our highest good as well as the highest good of everyone that is affected by our decisions.

When we operate solely through the lens of the ego, we are self-centered, looking solely at what we can acquire. When we are centered in our higher selves, we are Self-centered, always looking at what we can give. Helen Keller instructed us: "No one has a right to consume happiness without producing it."

We are not trying to crush the ego. Like everything, it's a part of the whole. Our goal is to reduce its influence and to hear its voice as just a small part of us instead of as the only voice. When we are in a state of flow, the ego's logical mind becomes like a hammer that is picked up when needed and then put down. Decisions are made from a higher place within us, and then we use the thinking mind to figure out the logistics which are needed to implement the decision.

MAIN TAKEAWAY

The ego operates solely from fear and has its own agenda, which is not one that serves our highest good.

 In what ways can you better limit the influence of the ego and allow your spirit to come to the forefront?

"*They must often change, who would be constant in happiness or wisdom.*"

CONFUCIUS

TWELVE

ACCEPTANCE AND CHANGE

W HEN WE RESIST CHANGE, WE WILL BE FEARFUL. WHEN WE judge ourselves, we will also be fearful.

Thus we must accept ourselves as we are right now in this moment, *while* desiring to improve ourselves and make changes.

It sounds very paradoxical, doesn't it? Well, existence is one big paradox. Nothing is outside of unity, and even the things we deem as "negative" like fear are contained in the whole and must be seen from that perspective. Being a fully self-aware individual is actually pretty simple. It just means that we have no self-judgment, and since we won't be projecting self-judgment outwards, this also means we will have no judgment of others.

The paradox was one of the hardest concepts for me to grasp, as it's not something we can understand with our mind. It has to be experienced to be understood. I always wanted to veer to one side of the paradox or the other, but I finally figured out that I had to energetically balance myself in the middle.

In order to heal, we have to look at ourselves and recognize what we believe to be our shadow or "darkness." But we can't stay there forever, and some use ongoing therapy or other healing practices to justify their state of victimhood and why they refuse to claim their power. The shadow is actually part of the light, and until we see it that way and see it beyond the field of duality, we will be forever trapped in trying to heal it.

Psychology is very important when we are in the self-discovery phase, since we are unaware of our beliefs and how they affect us. There is something to "fix." But eventually we have to rise above the belief there is something to "fix." The more we believe in the shadow, the more we energize it, and the more we think we have to work on it. Because we are looking at it wrongly, we can never reach the goal and this engenders fear. Although we start out seeing the shadow as we unwind our false beliefs, eventually uncovering our belief that the egg is cracked leads us to see that the egg was never cracked. This is the unity and wholeness to which we eventually return.

To come into a full awareness of who we are and let fear go for good, we have to eventually stop seeing ourselves as separate parts, such as our "inner child" or our ego. These exist in the same way that our liver or brain exist and interact as part of an integrated whole in the body, but they cannot exist separate from the whole body. With fear, the vast majority push it off because it doesn't feel good, which is a natural response and the same one I had. But the way to "get rid of it" is it to accept it as a part of ourselves and to welcome the lessons it's trying to teach us.

I went through a lot of therapy for my abuse, and this helped me to see the false beliefs and shadows I was suppressing and hiding behind, which was a tremendous blessing. But at some point, I recognized that everything I deemed as "negative" and tried to distance myself from was actually part of me. My judgment of these patterns and parts was causing me to see myself as fractured. Only through a recognition of my unity, even while still holding old patterns and beliefs that didn't serve me, could I come fully into who I am meant to be, which includes having no fear.

I may always be affected by my abuse and it may cause me to initially have thoughts or even to react, but I can quickly recognize these and not allow them to take hold of me, and I can always choose not to act like a victim. My abuse is no different than my propensity to hypertension. Having certain experiences and certain genetic patterns is *part of* our wholeness, not something which prevents us from being whole.

I have seen many people in denial, and I caution you not to take the above words and think you have worked on yourself if you haven't, as some try to spiritualize everything or say that what happened to them was not that bad or that it didn't affect them. These are just forms of defense that many use to fool themselves so they can avoid actually looking at their shadow and suppressed beliefs.

It's the same *collectively* with our shadow. Helen Keller stated, "It is wonderful how much time good people spend fighting the devil. If they would only expend the same amount of energy loving their fellow men, the devil would die in his own tracks of ennui."

What we energize, we bring to us, and it's often what we fear. Our collective shadow comes out in society through marketing, pop culture, and movies, as well as areas like sports where violent sports such as MMA and pro football continue to rise in popularity.

The paradox shows us we must accept things as they are, not fight against them, while wanting and implementing change. When we fight against something that is false, we give it energy and make it appear to have validity.

Change within both the world and ourselves is the only constant. We must feel comfortable with it or it will overwhelm us. The Greek philosopher Heraclitus said, "Change alone is unchanging."

The weather changes every moment. We accept this and we don't judge it. Yet we resist and judge the changes that happen with us, even though we are like the weather.

Change happens whether we want it or not, so we might as well flow with it as it will make the change much easier. This lesson has been brought to us in a big way with the coronavirus. We can float down the river of life effortlessly, allowing the current to take us where it wants us to go, or we can fight the current and be bashed against the rocks. Most of us fight the current because we are in fear. We don't trust, and we try to control the outcome of a situation. When we resist, we suffer.

In everything in life — our individual relationships, groups or communities, and businesses and ventures — flowing with change is critical, or the relationship, community, or business will eventually decline. This means having *no* immutable plans or expectations of where a situation needs to go.

Being accepting of change comes from having a strong faith. This is especially important around the journey that we are now on with the coronavirus, as we don't know where this journey is taking us. But we can have faith that individual and collective changes are in our highest good and will bring something better, maybe something we can't even yet envision.

Faith assures us that change brings renewal, and this is what happens in nature, which is our perfect teacher. Everything dies to become sustenance for the next cycle. Winston Churchill stated, "To improve is to change; to be perfect is to change often." Nature changes often, which is the natural cycle of life. Change always appears messy as there are no clean delineations between the old and what becomes the new — just look at what the caterpillar becomes in the cocoon.

I always get a chuckle out of seeing so many people try to keep perfectly manicured yards, as this is completely against the natural flow of life and we have to use major hacks such as poison. Have you ever seen anything like this in nature? Just look at a forest where everything is constantly decomposing to create the new. It's very messy. When we allow ourselves to join the natural flow of life and accept the messiness of life changes, surrendering to them, the most amazing things happen. We become the butterfly.

This is what the Universe presented us in the form of the coronavirus, as individually and collectively we were placed in a state of shock where everything we knew and believed was uprooted. If we are planting a garden, we have to first uproot the weeds before we can plant something new. The dying off of the old that does not serve us and the coming in of the new can feel scary because we have to trust in the process, knowing that we will harvest a bountiful and healthy crop.

The coronavirus has proved fearful for most — not just the fear of being exposed and getting sick, but also the fears that arise from experiencing emotions, attachments, and false beliefs about ourselves that have been buried for a long time. This has been a messy time emotionally and energetically, but again this is how a caterpillar becomes a butterfly — if it doesn't resist the process.

Acceptance of ourselves and change also means being present with our emotions, honoring them, and having compassion for ourselves as we allow what comes up to be felt and released *without judgment*. For we will not change these patterns overnight, but having compassion on ourselves, while we are working to change them, is the *most* important thing we can do to change them because this takes us out of self-judgment. This leads to great wisdom and internal peace. It's the Dalai Lama who said, "We can never obtain peace in the outer world until we make peace with ourselves."

When we accept ourselves as we are, we will accept others as they are. Fred Rogers tells us our task: "To love someone is to strive to accept that person exactly the way he or she is, right here and now." Accepting someone as they are means looking with non-judgment and seeing beyond the appearance of dysfunction to the spirit within. Paradoxically, when we accept others as they are and don't try to change them, this often creates change in them, because if we see them as the spirit they truly are, this lights the way for them to recognize this within themselves.

Seeing others as they truly are doesn't mean that we always approve of their choices, but we recognize that they are also going through great changes and have the right to make their own choices. This doesn't change who they fundamentally are. Certainly, we may be in a setting such as a business, where someone is not doing their job. Or we may be in a family where the behavior of one spouse is harming the children. We can be compassionate and kind while being firm about changes that are needed in their behavior.

We must accept who we are in this moment and accept who we are in the next moment, for we are constantly changing and constantly being renewed in mind, body, and spirit. By accepting the "new" you in each moment, you are affirming the real you that is behind all appearances.

There is a tremendous amount of change happening in the world right now, and this can be good. Change can be our friend if we allow it to be. In order to not be in fear, we have to really let go and trust that a higher power has us, our life, our loved ones, and really everyone on the planet.

MAIN TAKEAWAY

We can't change anything until we first accept it as it is.

What change do you fear most? Why do you fear this particular change?

> *"To fall in love with God is the greatest romance, to seek Him the greatest adventure, to find Him the greatest human achievement."*

ST. AUGUSTINE

THIRTEEN

A RELATIONSHIP WITH A HIGHER POWER

Many don't recognize and some even actively reject a relationship with a higher power. You can choose to pass on reading this chapter and you won't get any less out of the book. Well, maybe a little, but I understand fully and I won't judge you in the least. I greatly respect your choices as I know you would respect mine.

There are several reasons this chapter is important. First, as we discussed in energetics, everything is one unified field of consciousness, which is what is meant by God is One. God is the *only* reality. Gandhi stated this precisely when he said, "God is, even though the whole world deny him. Truth stands, even if there be no public support. It is self-sustained." Not mentioning God or a higher power in a book on fear and how the Universe works would be like describing how a car works without discussing the power source and whether it's gas or electric.

Second, there are such great misperceptions around this concept of a benevolent force, and these misperceptions have prevented people from accessing this help. This power has been of immense assistance to me and a great source of love, peace, and joy. I hope that I can provide some insight so that there exists the potential for this force to be an asset to you in lessening fear and in getting the right guidance in all areas of your life, especially in the times we are in where many are not grounded and may be inclined to panic.

Finally, even if we don't have a personal relationship with this force that I call God, we can be godly. If we are to live without fear, as well as change the current paradigm in the world, we must all exhibit kindness, respect, compassion, and integrity. We must recognize that we are part of one humanity and in this crisis together.

Let's first start out with this name dance between God and a higher power. As you may have noticed, I have not yet used the pronouns He or Him. Just my using the name God or Him will turn certain people off because of their conditioning or preferences, as would using higher power (or Divine Intelligence, Lord, Creator, She, etc.), but I have to use some pronoun or label to identify this consciousness that underlies all.

Unfortunately we have already lost something in understanding God's essence when we use a label, something Friedrich Nietzsche captured when he said, "Words are but symbols for the relations of things to one another and to us; nowhere do they touch upon absolute truth." Jesus used "Father" because he lived in a patriarchal era, and this was the best term that enabled people to be the most receptive based on that culture and the level of understanding of those to whom he was ministering. So the first thing I ask is that we all recognize our biases around something as simple as how to identify Him (and that pronoun is what I'm choosing to use, but I would be fine with using any of the other names).

This simple name conundrum points out what we have done to God as there is great controversy around Him. He elicits great devotion and love, but also resentment, bitterness, fear, and anger. We humans are the ones who have labeled God, put Him in a box when He is unlimited and undefinable, and created all kinds of dogma, creeds, and rules around Him. We have completely misrepresented Him. He is actually not controversial, but we have made Him appear controversial.

There are as many views about God as there are stars in the Universe, and many are badly misguided. Just as we mentioned with Truth, one religion or individual cannot have the "right" view of God where all others are wrong. God doesn't take sides. There isn't my God and your God. There is only *our* God, one God, who loves us more than we can possibly conceive and of whom we are all a part. In our world, change is the only constant, and yet this too, is an appearance. Underlying this appearance is a reality that is changeless, which is God and His love. It is our views about Him that change. We cannot fully know this changeless aspect in this world of symbols and shadows.

God is not a body, nor is He male or female. He is spirit that is everywhere and in everything (the Alpha and Omega), and we are also spirit as we are created in His image and likeness and are part of

Him. Western religion was created as a patriarchy by men who had egos and wanted us to go through them to reach God. Consequently, most think God is male, since we use the term Him, but God as spirit encompasses a perfect mix of masculine and feminine attributes. We too are called to reflect this perfect mix.

As Jesus told us, God is Love, and this is an unconditional love that we are meant to both receive and give. "You shall love the Lord your God with all your heart and will all your soul and with all your mind."

Unconditional means without conditions. *There is nothing we can think, say, or do which will make God stop loving us.* It is our self-judgment *about* what we think, say, and do that cuts us off from the recognition of our divinity, His love, and His presence within us. There is no type of penance, confession, or spiritual practice we have to do to reach Him as there is no separation between us and Him.

It is our false beliefs about sin, separation, judgment, punishment, guilt, and fear which prevent us from feeling His presence fully. We can't truly say and believe that He is Love, but also believe He will judge and punish us, as these are incompatible. Life brings us learning opportunities that we resist because we don't want to let go of our beliefs. Then we believe that we are being punished for some perceived sin by some deity that is in a faraway place. So we judge Him and assign false qualities to Him as if he were a human parent — often our human father, who may have been very judgmental and punishing but was trying to love us in a dysfunctional way at the same time. Our false beliefs about God can lead to a downward cycle. When we don't feel God's love, we self-judge, some to an extreme degree, and this often leads to people taking actions that aren't in alignment with their divinity.

If God has any judgment of us, it is judging us as His most holy child, of whom He is very proud and with a love that goes beyond anything we can imagine. Again, using words to label anything, like just the term judgment, leads us astray.

These false attributes that we assign to God are represented in the way the world works. For instance, we have a strong belief that people should be punished when they "sin," with a corresponding massive correction and prison system. I am not saying that in some cases someone should not be incarcerated, but certainly there are other ways of redemption for the majority. Or when I mentioned earlier in the book about the marketing of the legal industry, this doesn't mean that no one should sue another person as that may be the best course of action *based on the world we live in.*

But the system and the way the world operates is not something we should accept. The person or organization that commits a wrong should take responsibility and make amends instead of having to be sued. Without personal and collective integrity, we have nothing. If we trace back the false beliefs of how we have arrived at this point, it brings awareness to the fundamental problem, which is a belief in separation and the belief that God wants to punish us, and that some of us are victims.

I have had a push-pull relationship with God as I was pulled in by His love, but due to my self-judgment, I had a belief that I should be punished, and I projected that on to God as a punishing parent. So I pushed Him off and feared Him, but simultaneously I deeply yearned for Him. Many of us hold conflicting beliefs about God. Intellectually I knew what was occurring, but it didn't help until I was able to clear my beliefs that I should be punished.

Because we have projected false attributes on to Him, many of us fear God. In essence, this is also fearing ourselves. We are afraid of the light within. Plato said, "We can easily forgive a child who is afraid of the dark; the real tragedy of life is when men are afraid of the light."

How were we created? Are we just some random coming together of biological elements, and then we are gone when we die? If we are not able to trust that there is some force that wants only our highest good and loves us beyond anything we can imagine, then that can be a very sad and scary way of going through the world. No wonder so many people are fearful, anxious, angry or depressed. The last thing God wants is for us to live in fear.

Many people are lonely. God desires communion with us, as this is why we were created. We were created by Love to be loved, and each of us has this deep longing for communion with Him, although few recognize this. Communion means both a direct relationship with Him and a relationship with others, as we are each part of Him, and we reflect this to each other when we are present and have meaningful connections. This is obviously so with our family relationships and lifelong friends, but also just in a passing encounter where we feel a deep connection.

Communion with God completely and instantly washes away fear. "Don't fear, for I have redeemed you; I have called you by name; you are Mine" (Isaiah 43:1). There are numerous times in the Bible when we are told to "fear not."

When our longing for God is not fulfilled and we believe we are separate from Him, we try to compensate for it with the accumulation of toys and trinkets, and also with addictions of all sorts. But we cannot fill this need for communion with anything other than God. The high we get from eating or buying things, porn, using alcohol or drugs, or excessive exercise is temporary and only puts us in a deeper hole of depression, where we buy more or use more in an unsuccessful attempt to up the ante. The high we get from communion with God *is completely natural, safe, beyond anything we can imagine, and never goes away.*

God is both immanent and transcendent. The latter is the intelligent and organizing force that made the Universe. The former is the personal beloved relationship we have with Him in communion that makes our heart sing.

In communion we *experience* God — we don't *think* Him. Thinking God is like reading about skydiving versus actually doing it.

Words are linear, and they come from an ego mind. By nature, they are not Truth. God cannot be defined or understood through the linear and the language of the mind.

Another way of saying that we can't think God is *not* to say that we believe in God, because belief implies there is something "outside" of ourselves to believe in, and nothing is separate from the whole. Carl Jung described this well: "The word belief is a difficult thing for me. I don't believe. I must have a reason for a certain hypothesis. Either I know a thing, and then I know it — I don't need to believe it."

God can only be understood, and we can only be in communion with Him, through the language of the heart. Helen Keller explained: "The best and most beautiful things in the world cannot be seen or even touched — they must be felt with the heart." Our path back to God is through the heart, which is where God resides. It is through love. As we express love, we are expressing creation and God in action.

It is built in that we are meant to experience God and be in constant communion with Him as we live and have our being in Him, but we are so tilted to the ego mind that the vast majority only think Him. Then they make all these pronouncements about Him that are not based in reality.

These pronouncements and writings are complicated enough to make your head spin, with deep eschatological meanings. I am using that term to show a complicated ego label that only those who are *thinking* God can understand. So this is how the ego mind operates, since staying in the mind is used as a defense to actually being in communion with Him. These writings attract others who are similarly in their ego mind, but it is one of those "emperor has no clothes" deals where everyone is being fooled.

Does theology need to be argued? Do we need to know the exact specifics of what Jesus did 2,000 years ago? Do we need to discuss what the Trinity means as this reinforces a belief in separation? Just like with ourselves, we don't need to see God as parts. It's time to fully embrace our unity with Him and all of creation.

There are many seeds of Truth in religious texts, but we must also realize that the writers of these texts often did not meet the prophet or spiritual master they were writing about. For instance, with the Bible the authors of the four Gospels can't be confirmed, and these accounts of the life of Jesus were likely written many years after his death. They came from oral tradition which had been passed down. Also, there were competing sects of Christianity in those early years, so a writer may have filtered the message in a certain way to influence others.

Even if the author of the text is the person receiving the revelations, what they have been given is still being interpreted and colored through that particular human vessel. So we can't take anything literally. When we do, we are placing the letter of the law above spirit like the Pharisees did. We can only understand and resonate with the teachings and life of Jesus or those of any prophet or past spiritual master through the lens of our own journey of introspection, remembrance, and willingness to be shown Truth. What speaks to us at a deep level?

All kinds of false attributes have been projected onto God. Religious fundamentalists and those who fervently don't believe in God ("fervently" defined as those who want to force others to see it their way) have an inaccurate understanding of God, seeing Him as a ruler, in a body, who makes arbitrary decisions and is in some faraway place. *They see God and everything as separate, and this is false.*

The nonbelievers are really not nonbelievers, as everyone believes in some thing, some god they have given their power to through their belief. The fervent nonbelievers have made the *antithesis* of the God of religion their god, and they strongly defend this concept. They want to disprove others who do believe, and they try to do this by using religion and its statements about God as an excuse to deny the existence of a God who would punish us and allow children to suffer. How could a loving God allow this or something like the coronavirus? Thus He must not exist.

The opposite of this are those religious fundamentalists who say that the coronavirus is God's punishment on people for same-sex marriage and other things *they* don't approve of.

Both of these vastly different views might be logical if either were based on a true starting premise, but they are not. The starting premise for both the fundamentalists and those who have no belief in God is that everything is separate, including God, and this is not true. Thus everything that follows this false premise is also false.

God is not separate and doesn't make decisions in the way we think. Because God expresses through us, when we suffer, God experiences that suffering, but this is not what He wills for us. His will is only joy, peace, and love.

We have free will and individually and collectively we have created the world we see. If this is a world of fear, which it is in appearance, then it's an amalgamation of our individual fears, and we each have responsibility to change this. God will not override our collective will unless we are headed for disaster and we have total blinders on, but even then any action is done as love, never as punishment, because He does not punish. He only loves.

In addition to the religious fundamentalists and the fervent nonbelievers, another set of people who have misunderstood God are those who claim to be spiritual and who believe that only love and light exist, which is certainly true at one level of reality. But this is not the reality we live in. This is a kind of a "bury your head in the sand" approach, which means we don't have to work on ourselves or help the world (Jesus told us faith without works is dead), or that we can escape whatever is taking place. This is trying to spiritualize everything and deny our humanity, which is another type of defense against taking responsibility for our healing and how this can impact the world. We have to be present and grounded in this reality, *while* holding deeper realities, in order to be who we came here to be for ourselves and the world.

We also have spiritual teachers who have taken the sacredness of God and life and made it into a type of fast-food spirituality — a pill-taking mentality where everyone is looking for a quick fix whether that be their health, their healing work, or their relationship with God. But it doesn't work this way.

There are those who understand how the Universe works and offer prosperity seminars, charging a huge amount to give us the American dream, with little or no mention of God. Using Universal laws just to make money completely misses the point of why we are here.

It is apparent we have been conditioned from various sources with a false understanding of the true essence of God and why we are here. Jesus told us we need to be in the world, but not of it. "Render unto Caesar what is his and unto God what is His," is how we are all meant to walk the world as spiritual beings who are having a human experience. This is the true meaning of living in Christ, which means living in love. When Jesus said, "No one comes to the Father except through me," he was saying that you come back to God through love, which is the same as recognizing the Christ in you. Christ is God's son or daughter. Just as Jesus became the Christ through recognition of his divinity, we recognize the Christ within us and we reach our full potential as he did.

Jesus did not intend for people to worship him but instead to place our focus and love on God. "He that heareth my word, and *believeth on him that sent me*, hath everlasting life." Jesus came to be an example for us. He came to show us that we are divine and can see from a much higher perspective. We can resurrect or rise above our ego-based consciousness *while we walk the earth*. Sacrifice was something left over from pagan times that became a foundation of the story of Christianity to establish control and power through the priestly class, but God did not require Jesus to be sacrificed. Jesus allowed himself to be killed in his human form to show us there is eternal life and to show us who we truly are as divine beings and what we are capable of.

Jesus also told us the Kingdom of God is within, which means we can have this state of consciousness right now. Heaven and hell are states of consciousness. When we pass from this earthly reality, we move into a similar reality to the consciousness we carried while here on Earth. Jesus was referring to these many states of consciousness when he said, "In my Father's house are many rooms."

When someone comes back to a recognition of their divinity, this completely alters how they see things and how they interact with others and the world. Fear will be increasingly less present. Being born again is not tied to one religion or spiritual tradition. It simply means that we no longer live in judgment of ourselves or others, and we are not attached to things of the world above God. It is a complete mental, emotional, physical, and spiritual renewal that requires an immense commitment, perseverance, a strong love for God, and a total willingness to look at everything that is false in us and release it. This is why Jesus said the path is narrow and few will find it.

We are each on a different path of remembrance and understanding, which constitutes our journey. There are always higher levels of understanding and remembrance than where we are currently at. Recognizing this breeds humility and allows us to receive more revelation from God. Jesus spoke to us in parables because if we are in grade school, we can't yet understand calculus. We will have the key to unlock that hidden wisdom when we move into college, as we have experienced more of the journey and we have a higher perspective.

But we can also graduate with an advanced degree in any instant. The knowledge of who we are is within us. Our true essence is closer than our breath. We just have to release the false that's covering up this recognition. We are pretending to be something we are not. Let's be who we are. We are each a Buddha. We are each the Christ. Our holiness goes beyond anything we can comprehend.

When we see the false that we have made our god, this shows us what's blocking us from a relationship with God as He really is. The vast majority worship something above God. If it's money, Jesus told us, "It is easier for a camel to go through the eye of a needle than for a rich person to enter the kingdom of God." Or is it career, fame, approval, or even something like victimhood? We cannot straddle two worlds. Jesus said, "Do not love the world or anything in the world. If anyone loves the world, love for the Father is not in them." We are meant to enjoy the things of this world, but we can't make them our god. If we do, fear will result.

It's also important to recognize that God is our source of abundance, which includes financial wealth. If we believe that our job or something else is our source of abundance instead of God, we will be in fear because we have placed our faith in something that is false. And it's likely that the Universe will create a scenario where we must drop the false belief that our source is something other than God. Sometimes this can be painful.

If our perception of something is completely wrong, wouldn't it make us question everything else we believe? If I asked 100 fervent nonbelievers what it would take to prove the existence of God (an argument they use), I would get 100 different answers. Because in reality there is nothing in their eyes that would be satisfactory to prove God's existence. Christian theologian and philosopher Thomas Aquinas hit the nail on the head: "To one who has faith, no explanation is necessary. To one without faith, no explanation is possible."

Fervent nonbelievers use their lack of belief as a defense against looking at their overall belief system, and I mention them because this is a chapter on God, but this applies to any rigid belief system where someone is not open to the opposite view. The nonbelievers are no different than religious fundamentalists or fundamentalists around business, food, or technology. In reality, we all do this to a certain degree anytime we encounter a belief we don't want to give up. *And this creates fear.*

Beliefs are something we repeatedly touch on in this book because willingness to change them is foundational to any change that can first happen in us, and then in our community and business settings, followed by the world.

The need to defend our beliefs and prove someone else wrong comes from a great uncertainty in our own beliefs and sense of self. Especially now with technology, we join groups and identify with others who hold the same belief in an attempt to make ourselves feel safer and to somehow validate our beliefs. We think we can make what we believe true because so many hold the same belief. The more people who hold a belief makes it *appear* to be true — especially since what we set our intentions to, we create. But this is the dog chasing its own tail. We never step out of the illusion because it continues to reinforce itself. This herd mentality is also herd fear and has led to some of the most heinous crimes and acts against humanity, often in the name of God.

We have to label each other with a religious or political affiliation, or as holding some particular philosophy, because *not labeling* someone is scary. Not labeling them means we don't know how to deal with them because judgment is our fallback, and judgment and fear are the same animal. We want to label them so we can understand them, and either like them or dislike them based on the label we give them and how that aligns with our beliefs. *Until we place no label on them, we can't understand them as they really are in God.* What if we didn't label ourselves a part of any group, with no political, business, or religious or community affiliation, just a part of humanity and a child of God?

We only fight and become defensive against that which we feel threatens us and our identity and which we may feel to be true at some level. If we are completely comfortable in who we are, we hold beliefs but don't attach to them as our identity. We realize that our beliefs have changed and will change, and therefore we don't feel a need to convince anyone of our beliefs. If we feel led to share, we do this. We don't require the other person to accept what we say to validate who we are.

When we are fixed in our beliefs, we will be in fear. God cannot give us the information that is in our highest good such as information about the pandemic and what actions to take.

If we recognize that our beliefs constantly change and that life is a mystery, so that we don't truly understand anything, then we are really open to receive God guidance for ourselves and others because we have no preconceived notions that something needs to look a certain way. We all have our unique filters, but the divine guidance we receive can be much clearer with malleable beliefs than if we have a strong belief system already in place, as this clogs the filter. With divine guidance, we can be much more effective and balanced in all areas of our life.

Why try God? Why not? Is your life working smoothly on all levels? Isn't it logical to try a different way and to trust in something greater than yourself that always loves you and "has your back?"

This trust is not some made-up fantasy and is quite different from trusting in your job, the government, or anything of the world. If you speak to anyone who feels the joy, peace, love, and presence of God, they will tell you that this is the most real thing to them, and the most important.

They have the "eyes to see and the ears to hear." They know God through the heart. This is much more real than anything the ego mind can tell them. As all creation does, they praise Him, not out of obligation or fear that they will be punished if they don't, but out of pure joy. This is the Song of Creation that we have forgotten but which still resonates deep within us.

Our communion with Him is there for each of us because we "live and have our being in Him." Just like a ray of sunshine is not separate from the sun and a wave that appears separate is still part of the ocean, we live in God and He in us. Just like an individual rootlet that extends as part of the huge ecosystem of an ancient oak tree, we have the strength of that complete tree and ecosystem which we can use and trust at all times.

Rumi emphasized this communion when he told us that "There is one thing in the world which you must never forget. If you were to forget everything else and remembered this, then you would have nothing to worry about; but if you were to remember everything else and then forget this, you would have done nothing with your life ... Remember the deep root of your being, the presence of your lord. Give yourself to the one who already owns your breath and your moments." Again, we live and have our being in Him, and He is speaking to us and in communion with us without pause. But few are still enough to hear Him and to feel Him.

In the end, everyone is just looking for the meaning of life, to be loved, and to love themselves. Only God can provide that unconditional love that fills all those needs.

St. Francis and St. John of the Cross told us of how much joy there is in God. St. John said of God, "He alone is my joy." Meister Eckhart stated, "You may call God love, you may call God goodness. But the best name for God is compassion." Godly people, who may or may not be religious, are very joyful, compassionate, and have an inner peace that radiates from them. Does that not point us to Truth? Do we not want that joy and peace? It can be really simple *if* we allow it to be.

When we love as God loves, it is much more than an emotion. It is a passion to give to those most in need, to be of true service, and to love without expecting or needing anything in return. This is also our God DNA and we can never be in fear when we are coming from this place. In her powerful and direct way, Mother Teresa told us that "Love is a one-way street. It always moves away from self in the direction of the other. Love is the ultimate gift of ourselves to others. When we stop giving we stop loving, when we stop loving we stop growing, and unless we grow we will never attain personal fulfillment; we will never open out to receive the life of God. It is through love we encounter God."

Through the passion of love, we reflect God in this existence. Because we have choice here, this is our task in this reality. In heaven everyone loves each other, but in this world of duality it appears there is both "good" and "evil." In this world of shadows, we must *choose the good, choose God, and choose love.*

As mentioned earlier in the book, I grew up Jewish and I had a Bar Mitzvah but I never felt any connection with God until my late 20s. I would have judged others who said they did. But God awakened me one day with a seed of love in my heart. Some 28 years ago, I was putting down our eldest child who was only two years old at the time, and I felt such overwhelming love for her that I knew love was the most powerful force in the Universe. My life has never been the same. I'm not saying it has been easy, because it hasn't, but I could not imagine having a life without God's deep love, presence, and help. For me it would be a very empty, sad, and fearful life.

Each of us will have our own experience or non-experience. But we really can't have a non-connection with God. We can have a non-experience, but the communion is always there. There are reasons we may not yet have experienced God, and that may be because He has chosen to not yet reveal Himself, or because we are resistant to His entreaties. If we ask, we will be given the answer to this.

Ultimately, we all want to know we are lovable by others, but especially by God even if we don't feel Him in our life. Many create elaborate defense mechanisms and illusory systems of thought because they believe, falsely, that it will keep them safe from being hurt. Or in the case of God, keep them safe from being punished for their perceived sins.

If anything in this chapter or this book makes us angry, this is a good thing, because anger points us to resistance within us. If we are courageous and look behind the anger, maybe examining why we project false attributes onto God, we can grow.

This book or anything that life brings to help us heal, can't help us *unless we are willing*. I have found that many on the far ends of the religious, political, and other spectrums are not willing, and you can see this in the divisiveness and blame that is everywhere.

Coming to God doesn't have to be complicated at all. The simplest and most powerful way to center in spirit versus the ego — the statement that covers everything we need — is to pray to God "May your Will be done. Not my will, but your Will." Then just be willing to follow what we are shown.

Fred Rogers puts our task very simply: "I think everybody longs to be loved and longs to know that he or she is lovable. And, consequently, the greatest thing that we can do is to help somebody know that they're loved and capable of loving." This may sound Pollyanna, but we could use a good dose of a return to innocence, joy, love, and God in today's world in each of our personal, communal, and business settings. We have lost our inner compass, and this is why we are in fear.

MAIN TAKEAWAY

Without God we are aimless. When we look to God for help, we will be greatly comforted where fear has a much harder time in entering.

Do you believe God is separate from you? Do you believe God loves you? If not, why not?

"Faith is a living, daring confidence in God's grace, so sure and certain that a man could stake his life on it a thousand times."

MARTIN LUTHER

FOURTEEN

FAITH

ONE OF THE GREATEST OFFSHOOTS OF A RELATIONSHIP WITH God is faith, and in these times faith is critical, or we will live in fear, which can be defined as uncertainty and the opposite of faith.

There is a great misperception about faith. It is believed that faith is built, as when "outside" things happen that build our faith. But our faith has been there from the beginning as we are one with God. It is similar to the sun being there even when it's covered by clouds or it's night. So we only need to uncover the faith that's there.

Sure, "outside" things are nice confirmations that we are on the right path, but these outside things manifest *because* we have faith that they will. St. Augustine powerfully stated, "Faith is to believe what you do not see; the reward of this faith is to see what you believe."

When we plant a seed in the ground, we have faith that with water, it will sprout. Our faith needs watering like that. We need only to trust that God has our highest good and that good things will come to us if we believe they will and we allow them to do so.

If we ask things of God from a pure heart-centered intention, they will be granted. Martin Luther told us that "All who call on God in true faith, earnestly from the heart, will certainly be heard, and will receive what they have asked and desired."

Pure heart-centered intention doesn't mean we are asking to win the lottery, as this is an ego request. It means we are asking to be of service, to heal ourselves and others, to spread love and joy. Paradoxically, when we do this, we will be given everything we may have previously wanted. Jesus told us that God wants to give us the Kingdom. This means His joy and peace, which is what we really want, but it can also include worldly abundance such as wealth so that we can be a vessel to give this to others.

Many people do not have faith that things will work out for them, their children, or the world. Such fear has risen strongly in these times. Our faith that God wants to give us full abundance and have us live a life free of fear should be as strong as our faith that the sun will rise tomorrow.

Without each of us having individual faith, collectively we cannot create a new world free of fear. Helen Keller said, "Faith is the strength by which a shattered world shall emerge into the light." Each of us must look at the reasons we don't have faith (often the same things that prevent us from moving into a deeper relationship with God) and release whatever beliefs (the clouds) are blocking us from feeling the full force of our faith.

When I was in some of the deepest holes of depression, fear, and grief related to my abuse, faith was what kept me going as I knew that there had to be a purpose for what I was going through and that there would be good things on the other side. I knew that God was with me, even if I could not feel His presence. I also knew that there were many human and spirit helpers who loved me and that I would be presented with the answer to any problem regarding my healing if I just asked. Faith gives us the assurance there is a solution to every problem in life, but the issue is that often we are not open to the answer because of a conflicting belief. The solution may involve a number of steps, so the problem may not resolve immediately and this tests our faith.

It is an ego belief that we are the ones who need to make things happen in life. Of course, we are God's hands and feet and need to follow through on the doors that He opens, but our task is only to prepare the meal and set the table, allowing Him to bring the people to dinner. We actually *impede* the miracles God can work in our life by trying to do too much, for this is not faith. Of ourselves we are nothing. God only needs our full willingness and trust that anything we turn over to Him will be taken care of. When we completely get out of the way, we will be amazed at the doors that open for us.

Ralph Waldo Emerson explained that "The faith that stands on authority is not faith." Faith is reserved for God. We can have confidence or trust in someone or something, like a governing authority or a health authority, but this is a different kind of faith. Trust of this sort can and will change in an instant based on someone's or some authority's actions. Remember, any collective such as a governing authority or a company is made up of many people with individual wills and egos, and this is constantly changing. Faith in God is changeless and eternal, always there and waiting to be revealed. No one can take that away from us.

In these turbulent times, faith is especially important in knowing that we are right where we need to be. This may change tomorrow, but we allow God and the Universe to lead, and we follow, in faith, one day at a time. If a change is supposed to happen, it will be presented by a recognition or a new door opening. The Universe is always looking out for us and showing us what we need to pay attention to, but most of us are constantly distracted. One positive offshoot of this crisis is that our distractions are greatly reduced, enabling us to hear these hints more easily.

When we are shown something that needs to change, we may have some fear around this, but this is normal as there is a healthy interplay between our fear and our faith. This interplay uncovers our faith to a greater level.

Patience and trust go hand in hand. When we fully trust God and the Universe that something will happen, we can afford to be patient because we know it will happen. It's only when we don't trust that we become impatient.

We need faith for all of our relationships. Faith is the acknowledgment of oneness and is a basis for forgiveness. It allows us to look not to the past and "sins" of the other person, but to fully be in the now and see them as who they are in God. This clears our relationships of guilt and any negativity.

MAIN TAKEAWAY

Faith is the grounding that creates what we want to manifest. When we have faith, we are certain, and this means we cannot be fearful.

 Do you believe that you will be provided for in all ways? If not, what are the beliefs that block you from this understanding?

"Gratitude is the healthiest of all human emotions. The more you express gratitude for what you have, the more likely you will have even more to express gratitude for."

ZIG ZIGLAR

FIFTEEN

GRATITUDE

B EING GRATEFUL IS ONE OF THE MOST IMPORTANT THINGS WE can do to release our fear. Gratitude and fear are two different energetic states. The former is expansive and opening, while the latter is contracting. The former opens up infinite possibilities for Universal abundance and growth, as well as for information to come into our awareness that we need to make decisions, whereas the latter closes this off. Again, we create what we believe and energize.

Whether we realize it or not, gratitude is essential to the success of anything we are involved in. If we are being successful, gratitude is already present in a big way. For instance, a business is not successful without people being grateful for their jobs and being part of a team, with sales people being grateful for their making a new sale, suppliers being grateful for their relationship and business, and CEOs and team leaders being grateful that they can impact others.

Gratitude is part of our God DNA as it is one of the engines of creation. This is contrasted with resentment and bitterness, which are the opposite of gratitude and cause us to contract in the way fear does.

When we are grateful, our energetics are wide open and we exist in a God space. We can feel this simply by thinking of something we were recently mad about, feeling that anger in our body. Now, think of something for which we are grateful and feel that rising, opening energy in our body.

Many people are so used to depressive and victim-based thinking that they never move into the space of gratitude, but this can be changed. We have to cultivate an attitude of gratitude. "When a person doesn't have gratitude, something is missing in his or her humanity," Elie Wiesel said. "A person can almost be defined by his or her attitude towards gratitude."

Just like with learning to play a sport, we need practice. We are reawakening deep energetic pathways until being in gratitude becomes automatic. Then we are literally in a state that feels like heaven.

We can always find something to be grateful for, even when we are in the deepest depths of negative emotions. Certainly, it can be gratitude for our family or friends, but it can also start at the most basic level in being grateful that we are alive and we are taking a breath in the next moment, or just that we can read these words.

I used to be a pessimist and had somewhat of a victim mentality. My wife and a good friend of ours would call me Eeyore, the character from *Winnie the Pooh*, and this was slightly amusing for all of us, but it bothered me and drove home that I did not want to be this glass-half-empty person for myself, my family, or the world. I was always looking at and worrying about what could go wrong instead of seeing, envisioning, and trusting what could go right.

I believe I took on this mentality from my mother, both genetically and environmentally, as she was very much like this. She was also an abuse survivor, but obviously she had not worked through that as she abused me. I also believe that aside from the regular genetic and environmental transmissions we all receive from our parents, there is a separate transmission of victimhood that is passed through abuse, especially sexual abuse, and it takes a lot to overcome this. But once I became aware, I was determined that I would stop the lineage of dysfunction with my family. Thank goodness my father was an optimist. He had polio when he was three, and this affected him the rest of his life. He was in a motorized cart for his last 30 years, but he didn't complain about it. We should all have this type of attitude.

My point in all of this is that I had a large resistance to even feeling it was okay to be a joyful person, but I got out of this rut through gratitude. This took thousands of times of redirecting my thought and energetics to feeling grateful in my heart and body for even the smallest thing. I was literally rewiring energetic pathways in my brain and nervous system, changing my DNA. We can all do this when fear arises. We are spirit creating and inhabiting a physical body, and anything is possible.

We take so much for granted. Look at the natural world and how beautiful it is with the varying shades of color. We have this amazingly vibrant blue sky that we can look up at and be grateful for all of the time. God did not create a monochromatic world but one of incredible richness.

We often miss the holiness in the simplest of encounters and experiences. A while back I was checking out of a Hampton Inn in Connecticut. The man at the front desk greeted me positively with an open energy. After he printed my receipt, he asked me if I wanted one of the Hilton chocolates, and he handed me a small bar of dark chocolate. He said that he sits around with his wife and daughters and shares the chocolate, tearing off just a small piece (it was already tiny!) and handing it to each one because there is so much flavor in just that morsel.

There is nothing remarkable in that simple story *unless* you are looking for the remarkable and holy, which exists in everything. We think miracles and the extraordinary only happen every once in a while, or to a select few or to those who go to a place like Lourdes. But the miracle is *you*, is God expressing through you, and for this we can be very grateful. To get a high, we don't have to use stimulants, travel the world, or do something on the edge such as climb Mt. Everest. The *extra*ordinary is happening every moment if we can just be still enough to pay attention. This is the high we seek. Emily Dickinson told us to "find ecstasy in life" as "the mere sense of living is joy enough."

In that encounter in Connecticut, God was speaking to me through that man. Because I was open and wanting to be a blessing to others, I was given a blessing for which I was grateful as I thought of how much this man loves his family and they have this simple but powerful ceremony which binds them. "Where two or more are gathered in my name," Jesus said. God is speaking to us through each person we encounter if we would just pay attention.

When we start simple with gratitude, this cues the Universe that we want to move down this path. It will assist us by helping to raise the energy. When we allow it — and it's surprising how many of us don't allow it and don't want it because we want to stay in the lower energies — there will be all of these additional feelings that arise like, "Wow, I am so grateful for this, so grateful for that." We need to go with this flow, for it will help us expand and learn to be more in our body and heart versus our head. Then we can remember this feeling and pull it up the next time we are in a state of resentment or self-pity.

When I was in the weeds with HUSO and frustrated over the normal course of business things, we would always get an email or Facebook post which said that HUSO had helped that person tremendously and how grateful they were that we had created the technology. Then I would remember why we were doing it, and how grateful I was that I had a part in something so cutting edge that was truly helping people. The Universe gives us reminders all the time like this. The system is really set up in our favor, for we are surrounded by love and joy. Maybe we don't like our job, but can we be grateful that it provides an income? There are many people without any income, especially during this present crisis.

We want to be grateful for where we are, while empathizing with those who are less fortunate, taking actions we feel led to in order to help such people. These actions can be physical or they can be energetic, such as prayers of healing and protection. When we are grateful for our life, we naturally want to be of service and to give of ourselves in some way. This is our God DNA.

MAIN TAKEAWAY

Gratitude is expansive and is the perfect antidote to fear.

 Write down everything you are grateful for, even things you consider as minor. Take a look at the full list and feel the gratitude in your heart and body, not just in your mind. Stay with this feeling and remember it so you can bring it back up whenever you need to.

> *"Our task must be to free ourselves by widening our circle of compassion to embrace all living creatures and the whole of nature and its beauty."*
>
> ALBERT EINSTEIN

SIXTEEN

COMPASSION

BEING GRATEFUL LEADS US TO COMPASSION ON OURSELVES AND others. Compassion is an offshoot of love. Where compassion is, fear cannot be. Just as gratitude is the opposite of resentment, bitterness, and fear, compassion and judgment are also opposites. Compassion expands our energy, whereas judgment contracts it. Compassion is gentle and forgiving. Judgment and fear are harsh and unforgiving. When we reside in compassion, we see errors, not sin.

As mentioned, when we are in a situation where someone is abusing power, we need to extricate ourselves if possible, but we also need to stay in compassion as we don't know what has led that person or group to this point. Staying in compassion is holding *our* power that no one can take from us. Thich Nhat Hanh said, "Anyone who is practicing understanding and compassion can exemplify true power. Anyone can be a Buddha."

Compassion helps us to see that we are all in this together. Thomas Merton, who was a Christian theologian, Trappist monk, and acclaimed author, put it beautifully when he stated, "The whole idea of compassion is based on a keen awareness of the interdependence of all these living beings, which are all part of one another, and all involved in one another."

Nelson Mandela, who could have fallen into non-compassion towards those who imprisoned him, said, "Our human compassion binds us the one to the other — not in pity or patronizingly, but as human beings who have learnt how to turn our common suffering into hope for the future." Compassion is a central leg of unity vision and the recognition that we are one.

Compassion is really putting ourselves in someone else's shoes and knowing that we might take the same action if we had been through the same experiences. Also, if we were in their shoes, what would we want to have happen? We would not want to be judged. Having compassion on someone doesn't mean that we condone the person's actions or words. It simply means that we understand *how and why* they may have arrived at the point they have.

The vast majority are in self-judgment, and this is what we are being asked to recognize and heal. Self-compassion is the single greatest thing we can do for ourselves and is essential for any advancement we make in self-awareness.

Can we also have compassion on the adults who have conditioned or abused us, as they were acting from fear? They were acting from the conditioning which had been passed on to them, including abuse, self-judgment, prejudice, and fear.

If one of our family members such as our brother has an

addiction problem, we would support and love him. We might be firm that he needs treatment, but we would not turn our back on him and we would extend compassion to him. This is how we need to look at everyone in the world who is operating from a space of unconsciousness and committing acts that are not in their best interest or the best interest of humanity. Everyone in the world is our brother and sister in as meaningful a way as a loved one in our biological family. We are one family in God and in each other. When we start to understand this, compassion will flow freely from us to those whom we previously judged and hated.

Compassion has been particularly hard for me, because I dealt with severe self-judgment. I really had to work hard to get myself in a space of compassion for others. Of course I knew that when I could not do that, I was not being compassionate with myself, as self-judgment and the lack of self-compassion are really the same. Again, look to see what you are projecting on the outside to see what's going on with you on the inside.

If we are dealing with some type of emotional release or healing of trauma, the specifics of that release become almost irrelevant as self-compassion allows it to pass without any attachment. Self-compassion and acceptance that we are okay and exactly where we need to be, plus that God has us, are foundational to any type of healing and foundational to being a conscious human being.

Life is holy and wondrous, and it's also hard at times. Some of this adversity relates to our process of coming into a recognition of our greater self, especially when we resist, and some of it is just part of life, as when a loved one becomes sick or dies, we are laid off from our job, or the world appears to be falling apart. Through it all, most people are hard on themselves and bump up against their own false beliefs about what they should or should not be doing, thinking, saying, or feeling. We are *very complicated*.

So this process of coming into a recognition of our greater self is one of great friction and difficulty, and then we add in the "random" life stuff that comes our way. But the difficult times teach us what we are made of and often we surprise ourselves. We are like a diamond that has been formed through great pressure and even then, in its rough shape, it needs to be polished. You can only polish a diamond with a super hard surface, which mirrors the friction life provides us with.

Because life has adversity and we have the ability to make choices that align with our divinity, this experience on Earth is greatly valued at a spirit level as it's unique versus heaven where love and unity abound. As Jesus told us, we want to recognize the heaven within this Earth experience, the love and unity that is behind appearances, even when we are undergoing difficult circumstances.

Self-compassion takes the edge off whatever we are going through. It eliminates self-judgment, which is harsh, and it moves us into a gentle and forgiving attitude. Forgiveness and self-compassion go hand in hand. When we can have compassion for ourselves, we will have compassion for others — and vice versa.

We have to actively practice compassion as for most people, especially men, this does not come naturally. This is because we reside in a judging mind instead of the heart where compassion resides. The Dalai Lama captures this in one of my favorite quotes: "If you want others to be happy, practice compassion. If you want to be happy, practice compassion." Before we have a significant conversation with someone, ask how we can come from the most compassionate space possible.

Regardless of the circumstances, we can stay in compassion and love, rather than fear. This is the power that each of us holds and that no one can take away from us. It will change our life if we stay in compassion and live from an open heart at all times.

MAIN TAKEAWAY

Self-compassion is one of the most important things we can do to keep us free from fear and in a high energetic state, create more of what we want, and ease any healing we are going through.

 What has been something you have greatly judged yourself for and how can you see it from a larger perspective where you can now apply self-compassion?

> *"The weak can never forgive. Forgiveness is an attribute of the strong."*

MAHATMA GANDHI

SEVENTEEN

FORGIVENESS

FORGIVENESS IS THE BASIS OF DIVINE LOVE. IT IS THE ENTRYWAY which enables us to get beyond our ego's control, so that our spirit comes to the forefront. For the ego says that it has been wronged and that forgiveness isn't warranted. It never varies from this script, although the reasons for being wronged vary considerably. As we discussed in that chapter, the ego always has indignant anger.

Forgiveness helps us see the unitive "we" as opposed to "us versus them." The latter is where fear arises. Fortunately or unfortunately, the world gives us many opportunities to practice forgiveness as many are wrongly treated or judged. Even when this is not the case, we tell ourselves it is, and thus we still need to forgive as a means of reducing our vengeance and anger thoughts. Welcome these opportunities.

Forgiveness is gentle (can you see the pattern of how everything of God is gentle?). Forgiveness looks past the action to the God within that person and sees that they may have acted from a place of unconsciousness or they would not have taken the action or said the words they did. Have we not all done the same thing? Have we not said things or done things we wish we could do over? We have, and we should offer forgiveness to ourselves, which helps us offer forgiveness to others.

Jesus forgave those who crucified him. Surely we can forgive those who have wronged us. Surely we can forgive God for the false beliefs and sins we have laid upon Him. Yes, it is important to forgive God.

Non-forgiveness is a type of fear and a disconnect with ourselves. If we cannot forgive someone else, it's because we cannot forgive ourselves, and thus we allow fear to be our master. When we stay in this place of non-forgiveness, we are not punishing the other person as the ego believes. We are really punishing ourselves, preventing ourselves from feeling love. Martin Luther King Jr. said, "He who is devoid of the power to forgive is devoid of the power to love."

We are our own jailer. Have we considered that this person whom we can't offer forgiveness to is actually giving us a gift to help us see from a higher perspective and help us become more self-aware?

When we forgive, we are forgiven, because we are one. St. Francis emphasized our unity: "It is in pardoning that we are pardoned."

When we set our will to forgive, we are entering into a sacred covenant between that person, ourselves, and God. If it is an especially difficult situation, one where we may hate the person, we may have to work with our will and intention to stem the influence of the ego, which calls loudly that forgiveness isn't justified. But it is well worth it, as this is where our peace and joy lie. Energetically we are releasing the other person from the burden which we have placed upon them at an unconscious, or possibly conscious, level.

There is a powerful and ancient Hawaiian practice called Ho'oponopono that centers around forgiveness and letting go. We think of the person we have wronged or the person who has wronged us, which can also be ourselves or God, and we offer them this prayer. But it must be sincere even if we can only get into this place for the time we say the prayer. It's ideal for those we are angry with, because we likely want them to be punished.

Offering them our forgiveness is incredibly healing for reducing the power of our vengeance and other ego thoughts, as well as our letting go, which is so important for us and the other person. If we can do this prayer and mean it, we are warriors. We don't have to understand why or how it works — we only need to truly mean it for the time we say it.

"I love you.
I'm sorry.
Please forgive me.
Thank you."

Even though the prayer seems to be for those who we have wronged, it is as important to do it for those who we believe have wronged us. We have to be the ones who break the unhealthy energetic connection. Once we have forgiven, there's a large release and relief, and then the action or words the other person took are seen in a completely different light. It's almost as if it never happened. This is the power of the miracle of forgiveness.

When we come to realize how powerful our thoughts are and we think back to how many people we have affected with negative thoughts, words, and actions, and how many people have affected us, we may be utilizing the Ho'oponopono prayer a lot to forgive and reverse what we put into the Universe.

I have always pushed myself to get into a space to do the prayer, even though there have been many times when I have actively resisted. The reason I have done this is simply the release I feel when I forgive someone. It feels extremely powerful for me, and knowing how energetics and the Universe work, I am not in their body but know it is very powerful for them also. I would want someone to do the same for me.

When I have caused harm of any kind, I want to rectify it immediately because something inside me cannot live with it. I have also dealt with a lot of guilt around hurting those I love and others. We don't want to stay in guilt, as it's not of God — yet it can be an initial pointer to tell us that we have done something we need to rectify.

Maybe I feel a deep responsibility to be of service as a part of the whole. Anything I put into the Universe, even one thought of anger toward someone, has a powerful effect. I have learned to have more self-compassion (which has reduced the guilt) and to lower my expectations, as I am human and I won't get it right every time. When I feel I have fallen short, I say I am sorry or I will do the prayer if it seems more applicable.

MAIN TAKEAWAY

Forgiveness opens us to new perspectives and it allows for a release of both you and the person you are forgiving. Self-forgiveness is critical.

 As you read this chapter, there was one person who came to mind for you that you need to forgive. Be open to healing and try the Ho'oponopono prayer with that person.

"Integrity is doing the right thing, even when no one is watching."

C.S. LEWIS

EIGHTEEN

PERSONAL INTEGRITY

IT MAY SEEM STRANGE THAT THIS CHAPTER IS INCLUDED IN A BOOK on fear, but the two go together in a not-so-good way. For if we are in fear, there will often be a blurring of our personal integrity. When we don't hold to a certain standard of personal integrity, this creates fear in us and it becomes a downward cycle where we have less integrity. This creates more fear and a lowering of integrity.

It's as if we are constantly looking over our shoulder and waiting for the other shoe to drop. This goes back to energetics and how we each can feel how the Universe works, even if we haven't yet wrapped our heads around it conceptually and intellectually.

Jesus told us to do unto others what we would have them do unto us. His statement about not judging or we will be judged, which we mentioned earlier concerning projection, also means that when we do anything to others, we are doing it to ourselves, since we are one. Universal law is based on our beliefs, which create our reality. If we believe we are cheating and scamming others, we will also believe that these things should be done to us, which will place us in fear. Robert Louis Stevenson articulated this well when he said, "Everybody, soon or late, sits down to a banquet of consequences." The Talmud says, "Who is the wise person? The one who foresees the consequences."

Few people realize the truth about choices and consequences because it isn't evident. In heaven, we make a choice and it manifests immediately. Here on Earth, people think they can commit acts outside of integrity and get away with it.

In the short run it may appear that we have gotten away with it, since we have someone's money or we just feel righteous or better than someone we have judged. But every action or thought has a reaction, and these actions will come back like a boomerang because the same will be done to us in some fashion.

Integrity encompasses far more than our actions and words. Staying in hate toward another person or group, and being in a separatist view that focuses on "us versus them" — even if we never say anything to that person — has almost as much impact as if we say words to them or take action. The longer we energize a certain thought, the stronger it becomes and the greater the effect on both us and that person. We cannot stay in constant hatred or judgment and not have it affect us.

Again, we are part of a whole, so we are adding to the collective consciousness by what we are thinking and feeling, and this has a great ripple effect. This is why integrity includes cultivating our thought garden and pulling the weeds. It's important to not stay in negative emotions such as condemnation and hatred. It takes self-discipline. The Dalai Lama explains, "Whether you call it Buddhism or another religion, self-discipline, that's important. Self-discipline with awareness of consequences." This is a responsibility we share together as divine beings.

Self-discipline means that before we speak, we ask if this is something we really want to say, and we think how this will impact the person hearing it. So we have to not speak when angry, which is difficult for many people. Certainly we should not say harmful things through technology or social media, as if somehow these protect us from cause and effect.

I have improved a great deal in not speaking when angry, but I still fall short at times with my wife and sometimes with others as I want to be "right." We often fall short with those closest to us because it can be like two raw diamonds polishing each other. These individuals are the closest mirror for us. We also think that they will still love us regardless of what we say, but this is false and dangerous thinking. I have found that I will say hurtful things when I am feeling bad about myself and I try to project it off, or I am in fear. This has been my biggest regret with my wife although I don't stay in guilt. I recognize it as something that may have been part of my path to get to my current healing and awareness. But it's something that I would change if I had the power to, and I do have that power going forward. All that each of us can do is have compassion on ourselves and try to do better the next time. This is restoring our personal integrity and is all that God asks of us.

If you live outside of integrity, hurt others, or abuse power, you assist others who are not acting in integrity, or you are even part of an organization that doesn't act from integrity, there are consequences. You must remove yourself from societal herd mentality, including business and often your individual company's herd mentality, if you want to stay in integrity.

There were indigenous and specifically Native American cultures who would ostracize a tribal member who acted out of integrity, and that member would straighten up quickly because no one wanted to be excluded in any way from the group. But look at the groups we have now. These are not ones of unity like the above example, but groups who come together to uphold their system of false beliefs and who end up condemning others who hold the opposite belief.

This is especially true regarding politics and religion. Integrity is no longer valued. In fact, if you are someone who is eloquent in bashing another group or someone who has made a lot of money by being deceitful and ripping others off, you may be idolized and put on a pedestal.

When we are centered in God, we will act from integrity and do what is right, even if there are consequences we don't like or people judge us for it. Martin Luther King Jr. said, "There comes a time when one must take a position that is neither safe nor politic nor popular, but he must take it because his conscience tells him it is right."

The turnaround in integrity starts with one person at a time. It is personal and private, something we each do for ourselves because at some point, we realize that we can't be out of integrity and live with ourselves. It isn't done for someone else to see.

Once we have become aware of what keeps us in integrity, we must do it in every instance, or we are doing significant harm to ourselves and the world. We can't say it's okay this one time and we will do it differently the next time, because this is not a valid excuse. If we won't take a stand now, when will we?

When we purposefully don't stay in integrity, can we call this a "sin"? We can change and heal it the next time, but we have been made aware of something that is part of the divine order and we have consciously chosen to ignore it.

MAIN TAKEAWAY

Staying in integrity is critical to who we are individually and to removing ourselves from fear-based thinking.

 What practice or behavior do you do that is always in integrity? What have you done that you knew at the time or know now was outside of integrity? How would you do that differently if you could do it over?

"We are what we think. All that we are arises with our thoughts. With our thoughts we make the world."

BUDDHA

NINETEEN

HOW WE TREATE OUR MIND, BODY, AND SPIRIT

WE ARE WHAT WE THINK, EAT, AND DO. WE CANNOT ESCAPE ourselves. And we are multifaceted beings in many ways. If we don't recognize this and maintain all "parts" of ourselves, we won't feel whole and this will create fear.

Our bodies, every cell in them, are holy for they contain God's light. They are God's temple, and we need to honor and treat them as the amazing vehicles they are in this earthly reality, not as something to be discounted as some in religion or on the spiritual path want to do.

As mentioned, I have a major genetic predisposition to hypertension, so I have to be very aware of salt intake. This is not good or bad — it is just my unique expression that I am working with. Even if we have a lifelong physical disability, we can be grateful for the vehicle through which our spirit can have an expression as a physical body in this reality. If we see it the right way and understand our path and our lessons, everything can be a gift which brings us closer to God, even those things we see as "negative."

It saddens me when I look at people who don't appear to be taking care of their physical body, who eat poorly and have the accompanying health issues. It's likely their thinking aligns with this lower energetic as well. They appear as a shell of themselves when they can be so much more in God. Their potential is unlimited and they don't see it or refuse to see it.

By what we put into our bodies and how we treat them, we are respecting or disrespecting ourselves. If we eat junk food or food full of pesticides, we will limit how much of God's light can shine through us. If we don't get physical exercise, we will limit how much we can be God's hands and feet. If we stay up late at night on electronics, we are disrupting circadian rhythms that our bodies have been operating under for a long time and which we need for optimum health. Ideally, we are meant to go to sleep at sundown and awaken at sunrise, and this corresponds to the seasons and what we need holistically. Winter is a period of hibernation for nature and for ourselves, a time when we are meant to be dormant and still for the renewal in spring.

In the mental sphere, if we energize negative thoughts all the time, we have poisoned a beautiful tool which can be of service. With our thoughts we make ourselves and the world. By our words and actions towards others, we demonstrate how we feel about ourselves to them and to ourselves. We give to ourselves for we are one. If we want to be kind to ourselves, be kind to others. If we want to have joy, give joy.

We can't help others unless we are in a place to help ourselves. It is critical that we know what restores us and that we do these practices. Many people know what they need, but then they make excuses to not do these practices, the biggest being "I am too busy." When we know something is needed, we can't really complain if we don't take the time to nurture ourselves.

What can be universally restorative for everyone is to have time away from technology, which can be done each day, and time in nature, which may not be possible every day. But there are other practices that are restorative, such as yoga, exercise, meditation, or maybe beating a drum. Each of us needs to schedule that time in every day, just as if we had to take our child to school. If this means that we have to wake up earlier for this restorative time, and it means we have to miss our favorite show at night to go to bed earlier, this is what making our health, mental, and spiritual states a priority involves. We can watch our show on the weekend, but we can't get back that time we need each day to combat the stress we encounter.

I have always been good about making sure I frequently take restorative time. Some days that may mean only ten minutes of centering or prayer, but it's really my commitment to doing it that's almost as important as the actual doing of it. My intention signals the Universe that I am serious about taking care of myself, and this opens doors for people to come into my life and for additional opportunities to take care of myself.

With the quarantine and only being able to do my job in a limited capacity, I have had extra time to nurture myself, but it doesn't feel that way. I feel like I can't get to everything I want, and I have heard this from others. Important lessons are being reinforced about the true nature of time and living in the moment, and we are also being shown the false belief that we have to do a long list of things to somehow complete ourselves and be whole.

These are natural responses to shifting into a new energetic where everything is telling all of us to slow down. Previously, we were all running around and purposefully staying super busy, and now we are being forced to be still and take care of ourselves, learning what is real. We have to go to the opposite extreme of how we lived, which enables us to see the contrast. Then we can find balance in the middle.

With our health in all arenas, we can't allow the expectations of others to influence us more than necessary. Many in business have sacrificed health and family because of false beliefs and expectations that only they hold. Balance is critical. The Native Americans and indigenous tribes didn't separate work from leisure, as it was basically all leisure, even if one had a certain responsibility to the tribe like being the moccasin maker whose job had to be done for several hours each day. The concept of "working" sixty hours a week to make money to then use on finding joy and buying leisure would have been strange to them, for they were not looking for anything outside of themselves or their community. Everything we search for as a society, they recognized they already had, and this brought great joy.

Finally, we must speak to our spirit with some type of prayer or meditative practice. Connect to God. This can be as simple as a walk in nature or purposefully turning off electronics for 30 minutes and centering ourselves.

When we treat ourselves, our mind, our body, and our spirit with loving care and adoration, we will be given much in return and this will help us live free of fear.

MAIN TAKEAWAY

What we consume or don't consume, and how we treat our body, mind, and spirit, is critical to being able to be a full expression of God and to living without fear.

What habits or vices do you have that are holding you back from being fully alive in mind, body, and spirit? If you are working excessive hours, where did that expectation come from?

> *"Technological progress has merely provided us with more efficient means for going backwards."*
>
> ALDOUS HUXLEY

TWENTY

TECHNOLOGY

T HIS IS ONE OF THE LAST CHAPTERS IN THE BOOK, AND I BELIEVE I was guided to place it here because what we discuss in the chapter is meant to leave a lasting impression that stays with you. Our use of technology is strongly tied to our fear. This is also a chapter where I have included links because I want to impress upon you the depth of research around these issues and how technology is significantly affecting us in ways most people don't understand.

The benefits of technology, especially wireless technology, are undeniable. It has facilitated interpersonal communication and business in ways unimaginable even 30 years ago. Everyone loves their technology toys. But what are we not seeing, and what could this love of technology be costing us?

We look to technology for our safety and abundance as if it were a panacea for all of society's problems. This is a lot of faith to place in something that isn't part of the natural world. After all, can we eat computer entries in the event of an emergency? The US government passed a massive economic stimulus package for the coronavirus crisis with the push of a few buttons. It is kind of like magic, but do we want to place our faith in this kind of magic? This crisis should be a good wake-up call for all of us that unexpected things can happen, and have happened frequently in history, forcing us to see things in a different light. This includes technology.

To review, nothing of God is "good" or "bad." It just is. It's how we use it that is "good" or "bad." Does it bring us individually and collectively to a greater state of remembrance and recognition of our divinity, which will take us away from fear, or does it take us away from our remembrance, which will keep us in fear? Each of us must answer that question for ourselves.

It is evident that collectively, in a large majority of cases technology takes us away. It has been proven to be psychologically addicting, especially for children who have grown up on nothing else. The brain on a cell phone is the same as a brain on cocaine. It has also led to an increase in ADD-like symptoms.[1]

Before we had cell phones, the world didn't fall apart because a message wasn't returned immediately. I am old enough where I

---

1 https://www.forbes.com/sites/brianscudamore/2018/10/30/the-truth-about-smartphone-addiction-and-how-to-beat-it/#74cb433e4232

stopped at hotels to use the pay phone to retrieve messages from the receptionist at our business, and people didn't expect their message to be returned for several days. Now, people expect an immediate response and we have numerous email accounts and passwords to remember and protect. Many people have two cell phones. All software has to be constantly updated so that everyone has the latest and greatest, there are no vulnerabilities, and it all works together. (Good luck with that.) Most of us live in a constant underlying fear that our passwords and identities will be stolen, and of course there is a host of companies playing off that fear. They are responding to the industry of scammers that has arisen.

I was recently at a conference with a psychologist who is a big hiker. He was telling me that he had encountered some young people at a trailhead where three trails (a North, South, and West) intersected. They were confused by GPS and they couldn't figure out which was the North trail. The psychologist gently pointed out to them that the sun sets in the West and it was 4pm so that is how they could figure out which direction was North. How far have we come from the sailors who could navigate a vast ocean and small island destinations simply by the stars? We have lost the concept of sacredness that comes from working in tandem with nature instead of against her.

Energetics and technology are closely intertwined. For instance, there will be a significant difference between reading a physical book, which I recommend, or using a tablet. There will be a difference in how you take in and process the information, and a tablet cannot duplicate the look of the cover or the feel of the paper.

Before the coronavirus halted everything, I used to travel a lot and I was amazed at how few people actually read a physical book. Everyone was playing Candy Crush or watching a movie. Our brains need time to shut off from technology so that they can center in the moment. Just as we have an in-breath and an out-breath, and the sun rises and sets, there is a natural flow and cycle to life which we are meant to live each day. This involves downtime periods where we recover and rejuvenate. Periods of stillness and silence are vital to reconnection with our higher selves. Healing happens in the spaces between busyness. This is not possible when we are literally being pinged every moment by our devices.

There are other large concerns with technology, as it affects our health in many ways that we have not been informed about. We need the ability to make an informed choice as to how we interact with it. Our bodies and brains produce a frequency between 1-30 hertz (the resonant frequency of the brain is 10 Hz, while the heart is 1 Hz), and we have evolved over a long time living and sleeping in nature, which produces a frequency in the same range (the Schumann Resonance is around 8 Hz). We have become attuned to this Earth frequency which is grounding and helps us stay in balance in mind, body, and spirit.

Now we live indoors surrounded by fields of non-native electromagnetic frequencies (EMFs), and it gets worse every day in terms of coverage areas on cell transmissions, WiFi, smart meters, and other wireless technology. We don't think about it, and we don't associate it with our health issues because we can't see these EMFs, but they are affecting us greatly.

If you are interested in hearing and seeing these fields, you can download apps that will let you hear the level of EMF coming from your devices or from WiFi. Visit the link in the footnote to see some unique photos that visually show the strength of wireless signal by color.[2]

Again, we don't think about it because we can't see these EMFs, and most people assume that this is not a health issue or the government would step in. Bad assumption.

The FCC standards on cell phone health dangers are based on research decades old and address only the heating of tissues. They do not address what wireless technology does to the electromagnetic field of the body and how that affects health. Now 5G is being rolled out without any testing, and it operates at a different frequency band than 4G. Most alarming is that it relies on a large number of small cell towers that are placed every block, literally keeping us in this field 24/7.

Why does wireless technology affect health? It goes back to the understanding that everything is frequency. We are usually operating at a resonant frequency below 10 Hz, whereas a cell phone produces a frequency over *a billion Hz*. Is there any question as to why most people are literally wired these days, with nervous system conditions such as anxiety off the charts and over 80 million in the United States alone being chronically sleep deprived? When the electromagnetic field of the body is not in its normal state, it's difficult to be centered and peaceful. Even meditation becomes difficult. Fear is the result.

Keeping your cell phone next to your ear is comparable to putting your head up to a microwave oven that is on and has no shielding. This is why when you purchase a cell phone, the small print says do not hold it next to your ear.

2   https://www.electricsense.com/wifi-radiation-visible-device-emfs/

1. Jeremy Johnson has an excellent website that summarizes many years of research, including a recent comprehensive study by the US. National Toxicology Program (NTP) that draws a direct correlation between cell phone use and cancer.[3]

2. The World Health Organization (WHO) has declared cell phones as likely carcinogenic.

3. Hundreds of highly reputable researchers, health professionals, and even politicians have called for limits on wireless technology and additional research. The Bioinitiative Report was written in 2012 by some of these researchers and physicians. [4]

4. And since many who are reading this book come from the business world and understand risk management, here is some strong evidence on that front. In 2015 the insurance company Lloyd's of London implemented a blanket exclusion for EMF health-related dangers on all policies. Here is the exact language. "The Electromagnetic Fields Exclusion (Exclusion 32) is a General Insurance Exclusion and is applied across the market as standard. The purpose of the exclusion is to exclude coverage for illnesses caused by continuous long-term non-ionising radiation exposure i.e. through mobile phone usage." Lloyd's has been in business

---

3   https://www.emfanalysis.com/research/
4   https://bioinitiative.org/

for hundreds of years for a good reason. They understand risk and what is likely coming in terms of lawsuits.

I am barely scratching the surface on the scientific evidence, and there is also a tremendous amount of anecdotal evidence which can be found on the internet. Any reasonable person who is not in denial, or who is not working for an industry that benefits from wireless technology, would be concerned at what is contained in this chapter. Unfortunately many are in denial or have given their power away by believing that nothing sold to them could be harmful.

Television — the opiate of the masses. We have all seen the blank stare that happens when people look at television. This is not a positive blank stare. There are electromagnetic waves coming off the television, and it's also psychologically addicting with programming that is intended to pull us in.

Watching the news where everyone is blaming everyone else or where fear is promoted, and watching shows where there is violence, is not energetically good for us. These draw us away from who we really are and into an illusory world. We live in turbulent times and it's important to know what's going on so we can make decisions, but this can be done at a minimum level. When we're fearful, the fear feeds on more fear and entices us to read or watch everything we can, and this becomes a negative downward spiral where we can't rise back up from the fear. It's best to glance at the headlines and read the story only if there is information we really need to know.

It's evident that technology has connected us to a much greater extent in digital communities, but is this connection all good? Presently, with the current crisis, it is to a certain extent as people are isolated. But technology has reduced the need for us to live in physical communities, and it's in physical communities that we become grounded and form relationships we cannot form any other way.

In the indigenous communities, everything is a shared experience. Even in the agrarian communities or ethnic enclaves within cities, this was true until well into the last century. All of these communities came together in certain ways for ceremony, whether that was honoring a Creator, the planting of crops, the celebration of someone entering adulthood, or a marriage. Ceremony binds us, helping us to see our common humanity and divinity. As we have lost the physical communities, we have lost ceremony and the recognition that we are one, and this results in fear, judgment, hatred, and evil as we see ourselves as separate from our self and each other.

With each level of technology, we lose meaning. We cannot express ourselves over email or text like we can over the phone or video chat, but nothing comes close to physically sitting next to someone and having a conversation. Not only can we fully express ourselves without losing meaning because we can use touch, but there is also an energetic connection that happens and an ability to fully be present that doesn't happen through technology. We all know of the ways that people use technology to bully others and hide themselves on social media.

No one would argue that with each advance in technology, more things break and don't work together. So too much technology can negatively affect the energetics of any type of unit, whether that is a business or even a family.

I'm not asking us to stop using technology, as that is impractical. I am suggesting that we educate ourselves and cut back where appropriate, and that we take proper precautions in use of it such as using wired earbuds or using the speaker with our cell phone.

If we are in a position to authorize or push something like this to management in our organizations, it's best to hard wire. Help employees to understand and figure out ways to limit screen exposure and use EMF shielding on devices. They will be much happier and productive.

At home consider using ethernet versus WiFi or turning WiFi off when not needed, especially for sleep. Switch from a digital alarm clock, which puts off large EMFs, to a battery powered one and from a wireless home phone (another big field) to a regular landline. Keep cell phones off the body and in airport mode when not needed.

Equally, or more importantly, make a purposeful effort to go without technology for extended periods, especially cell phones, even if this starts at just one hour at a time. This is setting our intention to make a change and reconnect with that deeper part of ourselves, which we can't do if we don't have periods when we can be still and do nothing. If we go to the gym, we can leave the cell phone in the car and actually go old school and get something like a mini mp3 player on which we can only shuffle through the songs. We don't need to have our cell phone with its texts and emails, and we can allow the Universe to pick our music.

Technology is used as a defense against going within. "Be still and know that I am God." — Psalm 46:10. Many of us fear stillness and "knowing thyself" as we intuitively know we will meet a deeper part of ourselves where we have buried certain emotions and beliefs or patterns (our shadow), so we make sure we are always with people. If we are forced to be by ourselves, we are playing games on our phone, surfing the internet, listening to talk radio in the car, always on the go, or busying ourselves in some way.

As mentioned earlier, there is irony in the term "nonessential" being used for the current crisis. Much of what we do and how we busy ourselves from being still is nonessential in terms of our wellbeing. Much of what we have given our power to and how we see things outside of ourselves is nonessential to having a joy-filled and authentic life.

Even though I had already stopped being attached to results for my favorite teams before the coronavirus hit, I found myself initially checking my phone about once a day for free agent news on pro football since it was the only thing going on with sports. This was like a bad habit or a rut I was still in, and it was my simple way of trying to hold on to something that was going away or was at least being minimized for myself and the world in a revealing way. I can only imagine the withdrawal pains for those who were really attached to sports, often in an unhealthy way. As we have discussed, the Universe has a way of forcing us to look at what we have made our god.

We also don't want to be still because we fear meeting the God within us. With powerful words Mother Teresa tells us, "We need to find God, and He cannot be found in noise and restlessness. God is the friend of silence. See how nature — trees, flowers, grass — grows in silence; see the stars, the moon and the sun, how they move in silence … We need silence to be able to touch souls."

Finding God within us is the same as knowing ourselves. Chinese philosopher Lao-Tzu said, "Knowing others is intelligence; knowing yourself is true wisdom." Socrates simply stated, "Know thyself." This is the greatest journey we can make compared to anything the outside world can offer. Jesus in the Book of Thomas reinforced this when he said, "Whoever does not know self, does not know anything. But whoever knows self, has acquired the knowledge of the universe."

Earlier in the book we mentioned the gerbil on the exercise wheel not having a destination. Our destination is ourselves and the stillness we find within us. Stillness gives us the answers to our problems. Find your center, be in the present moment, and everything of the world fades away. Stillness will completely restore. It will give us a new perspective. In stillness we will find what we are seeking.

I used to hold a false belief that I had to get all of my tasks and everything out of the way before I could be still, but this was not living in the moment and it missed the whole point about stillness and God being within every task and every moment. This came from my belief I had to continually be achieving, a belief many of us hold, which meant I had to constantly be doing. Even when I was still, I sometimes felt guilty and watched my time.

Once we become masters of stillness and living in the now, we will be able to hold that stillness even in the most difficult of circumstances, even when we are using technology. We are like a deep lake that has waves from strong winds. The strong winds and waves are the world and what we experience every day. But at the bottom of the lake, which is our inner essence, it is undisturbed by the waves and there is pure stillness.

John Muir talked about the connection between God and nature: "Oh, these vast, calm, measureless mountain days, days in whose light everything seems equally divine, opening a thousand windows to show us God." Nature is the great equalizer as it can recalibrate our electromagnetic field and help us remember what is real versus the false paradigm that we collectively live in. We should strive to be in nature as much as possible, and we should not take our cell phone on our walk unless it's necessary because we have young kids for example.

Also, it's best to just listen to the sounds of nature over any music. We are actually hard-wired to respond in a calming and centering way to bird song and other nature calls as this was how we evolved for a long time. If the birds were singing, there were no predators in the area. Nature grounds us and helps us to remember who we are. Where possible, add outdoor and indoor green areas to corporate settings.

Please be especially diligent with children and technology as it's almost universally agreed that children are much more susceptible to wireless technology with their still developing brains. Even the American Academy of Pediatrics recommends no more than one hour per day of technology for kids ages two to five. Can there be any question as to why so many children exhibit ADHD symptoms when they are exposed to non-native frequencies virtually 24/7? (And then many are also eating junk food or food with heavy pesticide content.) Their behavior is not their fault. They exist in the world we have created. Please don't entertain a three-year-old with a tablet or phone.

When you are in digital overload and you are wired all the time and can't sleep, recalibrate your own electromagnetic field through being in nature or some other simple means such as taking Epsom salt baths, letting the water run on your head in the shower, or using HUSO sound therapy. When we recalibrate the electromagnetic field of the body to its natural state, we can access deep wisdom, and this is why so many people get revelations in the shower.

Now, before we finish this chapter, let's move away from the technical and consider use of technology from a quantum physics and spiritual perspective. Many scientists and others believe there are an infinite number of realities or dimensions existing at the same time, which is similar to the many rooms in my Father's house of which Jesus spoke.

Remember from the earlier chapter where we discussed how thought is creative. We literally create our reality by what we think. So when someone is using technology to a great extent, they are being sucked into a virtual reality world, one of their own creation and one that exists collectively. This is the case whether we are immersed in video games, spend excessive hours on social media, or watch porn. A *third* of internet downloads are porn, with a large number being teenagers of both sexes. *This is the world we have created* through our collective choices, and the symptoms of our collective illness are giving us a big wake up call.

This virtual AI world has far reaching consequences beyond the huge concerns mentioned earlier in this chapter, as we are becoming cleaved from spirit and separated from our own essence. Can we feel the difference when we engage with virtual reality? We should, as it's a totally different feeling than when we are swimming in the ocean or walking in a forest of large trees. This digital AI world is not one that is grounded in the frequencies of the natural world, nor is it likely that we are meant to become virtual avatars. We are all in a great state of flux right now as many of these alternate realities are very present and overlapping in this Earth reality. With many who have given their power to this digital reality, their appearance looks like they are in a different reality, which they are.

As we asked at the beginning of the chapter, technology has done many things for us, but *at what cost*? Is becoming more dependent on technology a sustainable path? Maybe the scammers, the constant upgrades, and the technology failures are symptoms. Maybe we are being told that this is not the right use of technology, and that it is not sustainable as we move farther away from the simplicity and beautiful working order of how God created us and the natural world. Spirit is what gives life to everything. Can anything cleaved from it continue to exist?

We have placed great faith in technology, but we can call this misplaced faith? When we place our faith in anything that is of the world, it can only lead to fear.

MAIN TAKEAWAY

Technology has given us many benefits in our personal and business lives, but it has health consequences of which we need to be cognizant, and it has taken us away from ourselves, from our true essence.

 What will you commit to starting today to limit your use of technology? Please don't tell yourself that it is not possible as that is not true.

"At the end of life we will not be judged by how many diplomas we have received, how much money we have made, how many great things we have done. We will be judged by, 'I was hungry, and you gave me something to eat. I was naked, and you clothed me. I was homeless, and you took me in.'"

MOTHER TERESA

TWENTY ONE

COMMUNITY

B EING IN A FORCED TYPE OF ISOLATION LIKE WE HAVE BEEN with the coronavirus crisis may not seem like a blessing, but it has forced us to be still and go inside ourselves. At the same time it has allowed us to see how we are truly linked as one humanity, for we are all undergoing the same experience.

Relationship with others is the primary vehicle through which we remember who we are in God. Our relationships reflect our communion with God, as does our connection to the natural world. We are meant to be social creatures living and helping each other as one community. Doing this through technology is better than not at all, but as described in the last chapter, it immerses us in a false world, and it's not the same as being in physical relationships in the natural world.

As shown by the Mother Teresa quotation, community puts us in a place to look after each other. Community and empathy are closely interlinked, as community means not only physical but also emotional support and bonding. The coronavirus crisis has naturally created empathy because we can understand exactly what most everyone else is going through.

When we are in community, we automatically fall into service to those in need because we know them and see their need up close versus judging someone from afar and condemning them. "Community" comes from the Latin for "fellowship," meaning "with unity." "Compassion" comes from the Latin "suffer together." We have a passion to help those with whom we share unity and suffering. This is our God DNA and will arise naturally with great joy, unless we have suppressed our spirit.

It has only been very recently in our history that we have not lived as family units. Many people have moved every few years for their career. My wife and I built our house almost 30 years ago and all four of our children have grown up in this house. When our children are in difficult circumstances, regardless of where they are living in the world, they can come back and sleep in their childhood bedroom. Sleeping in their childhood house is grounding for them and allows them to go back out and face a world which has become very tough. Before coronavirus, many in business chose to take new opportunities and climb the corporate ladder by moving every few years, which has consequences both positive and negative. Will this desire be as strong as we come out of this experience?

Many grandparents do not live in the same city as their grandchildren. When we lived together, the grandparents were considered elders because they had accumulated wisdom. While the parents worked, the kids were raised by the grandparents and other elders in the family and community. It was a system that worked well, and we had wise and open young adults ready to use their gifts for the whole. Now we have marginalized the elderly and stuck them in retirement communities instead of gleaning their wisdom and having them continue to contribute. Our society is paying the price. No wonder so many are depressed. Again, someone doesn't accumulate wisdom because they are a YouTube sensation, can code an app at age 22, or because they can throw a football well. This is popularity and adulation, not wisdom.

Community is also in our DNA. When we lived as hunter-gatherers, and even when we moved into agrarian communities, if we were kicked out of the group we would die. So we each have a fear around this. Many allow this fear to control them and do anything so they will be liked, including giving their power and authority to others. But we are being called to stand on our own two feet as well as to be part of communities in which everyone is empowering everyone else, and where love, respect, and gratitude are forefront. This is, we hope, what will come out of the crisis we are in.

The workplace is another community, but it's a critical one because we spend so many hours in this community setting. Ideally we will see many changes in this arena since it's disproportionately geared to separation and a profit mentality.

Thich Nhat Hanh said, "I love to sit and eat quietly and enjoy each bite, aware of the presence of my community, aware of all the hard and loving work that has gone into my food." Most companies are not preparing food together, but they are aligned in a common goal, hopefully one of making a product or doing a service that's of great help to others.

As part of this, CEOs and leaders must search for the elders in their companies and give them greater roles, giving employees the ability to access their wisdom, both business and personal. Maybe they can write blogs or have community gatherings. Business can be so much more in terms of reflecting the true nature of community and bringing us together as one.

Functioning, true communities understand that no one in the community is better than another and that everyone must be provided for. The queen bee cannot do her job or even be fed without all of the workers. Communities truly function as a whole unit.

As touched on in the chapter on gratitude, being of service and doing "works" for our communities can mean any number of things, from uplifting the world with light and prayer to showing up at a rally to providing financial assistance to one individual. All are important. God will lead you in the way you can best serve, and this may change over time. But we must do service from the perspective of "be in the world but not of the world." As we help others, we hold the highest perspective that we are all one and that those we are helping are not victims. They are temporarily experiencing difficult circumstances. When we see them as a part of God and ourselves, this will help them to see themselves in the same way, and this is ultimately the answer out of their circumstances.

When we consider something like reparations for historical wrongs, are we reinforcing the idea of separation and victimhood, and are those who are giving assuaging their guilt, which is also reinforcing separation? We can't change the past. What we can do is acknowledge that certain actions and perspectives in the past came from a separatist view, and this did not serve certain individuals, groups, and especially the whole of humanity. If we stay in condemnation, hate, and victimhood, aren't we creating a future that is the same as the past? We create a different future when we each become a vessel of love and compassion, which will raise the whole vibration of humanity and allow others to also recognize that we are one.

When we finally understand at a deep level that we are inherently one community, we will no longer see through eyes of separation and we will no longer live in fear.

MAIN TAKEAWAY

Community connects us and helps us to see from a unity perspective.

 What can you do to foster more community in your workplace or other settings? One candle can throw off a lot of light in a darkened house.

"Attachment is the great fabricator of illusions; reality can be obtained only by someone who is detached."

SIMONE WEIL

TWENTY TWO

NON-ATTACHMENT, PERFECTION, AND FREEDOM

WHEN WE ARE ATTACHED TO SOMETHING EPHEMERAL, WE will be in fear, whether we recognize the fear or not. We have built our inner house upon quicksand instead of a rock, and we will always hold an underlying fear that the house will sink.

Attachments or desires are different from preferences. I like strawberry ice cream and you may like chocolate. These are preferences. We aren't attached to a flavor of ice cream. We don't condemn someone else for liking a different flavor.

An attachment is something we put above other things, and sometimes we will defend it to our death. As previously mentioned, many in this society are attached to money or power over anything else. They have made these false idols their god and have placed it above God. Other people crave attention, being in control, avoidance of ridicule, avoidance of pain, and always being right. There are literally as many unique attachments or desires as there are people in the world.

Many are also attached to practices like meditation which connect us more with God and a greater reality. If there is a practice or ritual, inside or outside of religion, that speaks to us and brings us closer to God, we should continue to do this. Nature does this for me. This is our flavor of ice cream that we prefer. It is God's unique expression through us and how He brings us closer to Him.

But as we mentioned with psychology, we may have to let go of the attachment at some point in order to fully move into a unity perspective. These practices help us to feel centered, and we see them as better than when we are in anger or self-judgment, but this is a duality perspective. It's the recognition that God is contained within all, including those times when we are not centered, that finally allows us to release all fear and experience the immense joy that comes from unity. Jesus told us to pray without ceasing, but this does not literally mean saying a prayer repeatedly. It means that we should continually recognize God's presence within us. This involves approaching all of life as a meditation and holy ritual. We should continue to do the practices that give our hearts joy and center us, but we have to let them go if they no longer serve us.

The Universe will show us what we should not be attached to — that which is false versus what's real. Our spirit comes here for a purpose and doesn't want what's false. The ego is what *desires* the false. It judges and condemns those who don't hold the same desire or who haven't achieved that desire, especially in the case of money. But attaching to the false keeps us in fear. Buddha told us that "There is no fear for one whose mind is not filled with desires."

The attachment that is present in almost everyone, and is foundational to other attachments like money or power, is approval and caring what people think about us. This is almost always formed in childhood. We must release the belief that *what someone else thinks of us defines us.* This is ultimate freedom.

The problem is that we desire to be something we are not, instead of seeing the perfection that is already present. This is greatly reinforced by marketing that tells us we need this product or service if we want to feel that we are "complete." Collectively, we have a distorted view of the term "perfection," as it sets a goal we can never achieve and this brings fear. Many say that Jesus was perfect, but Jesus became angry — and the Dalai Lama says he has anger thoughts, too. Does becoming angry make us imperfect?

Ralph Waldo Emerson said, "Every particular in nature, a leaf, a drop, a crystal, a moment of time, is related to the whole, and partakes of the perfection of the whole." Maybe we are already perfect, yet we are also working towards perfection. Again, the paradox presents itself.

Since God is perfect, and God is all that exists, we are one with that perfection. Yet it appears in this world of duality that we can make choices to make us more "perfect." We can be less angry, more kind, more compassionate, more intelligent. But where does perfection begin and end? Maybe we need to reframe our definition of perfection.

We categorize and judge things through a framework of bad, good, better, or best. Through those eyes, it would appear that we can always be more perfect. But we would not describe a piece of art as perfect, any more than we would say that the way a bird sings is imperfect. Maybe perfection is found in God expressing in so many amazing and holy ways through each of us and through everything in the Universe.

Is God's expression through a developmentally disabled child any less than through a child with no disabilities? If we think so, it's because we have applied our judgment to this example. God's experience is no less holy in the developmentally disabled child. This Earth reality is just a place for God to have an expression in and through us, and for us to awaken and remember. Every single life experience serves this purpose if we allow it, and none is more perfect than another because they are all perfect already.

Jesus showed us what we can become. He showed us how we are meant to walk the world as a mix of our divinity and humanity. This means we may do things we regret, but we can make amends by doing it differently the next time. From this understanding we can relax into the perfection that is already there and have great compassion on ourselves and others when we aren't "perfect."

Letting go of attachments and seeing the perfection that is already there sets us free. We are free when we don't judge ourselves, anyone, or anything, and when we no longer look outside of ourselves for our identity and self-worth. We are free when we live in the present moment and there is no fear. We are free when we give back to life as much as it gives us.

As I mentioned earlier, I used to travel a lot on business, and I would see all of these business people having these intense conversations in person or on the phone. They were really into it like it had meaning in and of itself. Can we realize that we are in a game?

Just like the actor on a stage, we play our parts to the fullest, but we don't believe it's real. This is freedom. It allows a much broader view to enter, confers on us God's joy, peace, and certainty, and gives us the ability to be who we really are. We can make exponentially more powerful decisions as we are not coming from fear. We can continue to have these intense business or life conversations as before, but we can do it with the knowledge that there is a much higher purpose than what we are discussing in that conversation. *We get to choose how we want to play the game.* My suggestion is that we play it consciously, versus unconsciously.

Our goal is to strive to be free from all childhood, business, and societal conditioning. When we are there, we are an authentic and empowered individual who can truly change the world.

MAIN TAKEAWAY

When we are not attached to anything such as a certain outcome or what people think of us, we are free and we will be fear-free. This allows us to play the game with conscious intent.

Close your eyes and pretend, just for a couple of minutes, that you have amnesia and you don't remember who you are. You have no history. You don't know how old you are and even what you look like. You have just awakened from a long dream and you don't know where you are. Let that soak in and be present with it. Initially it may bring up fear. But when you get past the fear, you can get a sense of what it means to be fully non-attached and free.

"Do the thing you fear and the death of fear is certain."

RALPH WALDO EMERSON

TWENTY THREE

ALLOW
THE FEAR

F EAR FEELS CRAPPY. THERE IS NO WAY AROUND THAT. BUT MOST of us don't respond to our fear in a logical way. Anytime we bump up against long-held beliefs that no longer serve us and need to be released, which is what is being accelerated individually and collectively during this time, we will feel fear. We can choose to medicate it and suppress it, which won't be successful and the fear will only knock at our door more loudly. Or we can choose to face and heal the fear, welcoming its message and the growth that will come out of it. As Robert Frost said, "The best way out is always through."

Allowing the fear simply means that we don't run from it, nor do we dive into it. When a baby is in a birth canal and is being squeezed, she doesn't try to go back into the womb or stop the process of moving. She relaxes and allows the process to unfold so that she can get through the birth quickly.

Along with everything else that arises in us, we embrace our fear as a part of ourselves as that is the only way we can feel whole. We ask it where it originates from and what it wants to teach us. This is the natural response that is within each of us, but our ego minds override this and we have all of these subconscious beliefs that sabotage our healing and prevent us from hearing fear's message and healing from it for good.

In order to transform our fears, we have to recognize what we can control and what we can't. We can always control our ability to live from an open heart, to be kind, and to show compassion and love to ourselves and others. We can control our ability to stand in our divinity and not give our power away. We can also control our ability to love and trust in God, that there is a higher plan, and that if we pay attention we will be shown the actions we need to take. There may not be much more we can control. For the things we can't control, we have to first recognize what they are and then surrender them to God and know we have done all we can do. This may sound simple, but this will keep us out of fear.

Warriors still have fear, but they are willing to face their fears and work through them, which takes great courage. Nelson Mandela described this when he said, "I learned that courage was not the absence of fear, but the triumph over it. The brave man is not he who does not feel afraid, but he who conquers that fear."

One of the best ways to move through pockets of fear is to take whatever action we can concerning what we have fear about, assuming we know this is what's in our highest good. Dale Carnegie told us, "Do the thing you fear to do and keep doing it ... That is the quickest and surest way ever yet discovered to conquer fear."

Although I have been in a lot of fear, I have never let it stop me. I always knew that I had to take the action and push through the fear or I would never recover from the fear. The fear would win and be my master. Fear of staying in fear forever, and fear of not being the best husband, father, and human being I have the potential to be motivated me. Unfortunately, many people stay in fear most of their lives, but facing our fear will bring us heaven. Mythologist Joseph Campbell stated, "The cave you fear to enter holds the treasure you seek."

Taking an action to move through the fear could mean having a difficult conversation with our spouse or boss, starting meditation, going into therapy or rehab, putting more money into a venture that we know is doing good in the world but is still in the red (that was me with HUSO), or moving into a completely different career without a safety net.

Taking action can also mean non-action, like not giving advice to someone because they need to come to a realization on their own, even though we know that our keeping quiet could end up in disaster for them. If we are still and pay attention to what God is trying to tell us, we will get the action or non-action that's in the highest good for us and those around us. This is the quickest way out of fear.

We are called to move through fear at different times, as taking the action or non-action will peel back another layer of our beliefs so we can come more fully into a deeper recognition of our divinity, which is the answer to all fear. Marie Curie said, "Nothing in life is to be feared, it is only to be understood. Now is the time to understand more, so that we may fear less."

As we have explained, the problem that's least understood is that so many people have invested their identity in what is false, such as who they are in their job or community, how much money they have, or whether their sports team wins. Only by moving into the safety, identity, and love of God and a unitive perspective can fear be dissolved. We can love our career and do well in it, enjoy what money brings us, or enjoy watching our team win. But these things are not our identity or our god.

Gandhi told us, "The enemy is fear. We think it is hate, but it is fear." I mentioned in the preface that fear can be our friend. We have seen fear as our enemy because we have tried to run away from it, but it's time to reframe our perspective and see what it's trying to teach us. Again, it really doesn't matter what the external circumstances are. Fear is just an energy in the body. What it becomes for us is based on how we see and respond to it. It can be debilitating on the "negative" side, or it has the potential to be powerful on the "positive" side, releasing false beliefs and an immense amount of energy and creativity.

Although I know the opposite is out there as people are fighting over toilet paper and I can feel people's fear at an energetic level, one of the things I have noticed greatly with the coronavirus crisis is that there are bright pockets of cooperation and love, offers to help out those who can't or shouldn't get out, and more people being in nature. I am seeing these things *because* I am looking for and expecting them, and because I am open and grateful for the positive changes that this crisis has already brought in me and the world. Even with deaths rising, we can make lemonade out of lemons as this gives us the potential to increase our empathy, be there for others in need, and really see what's important in life.

Even with each of us being part of the whole and partially affected by the actions of others, we must recognize that we are truly the creator of our life. How we choose to see things and act will determine what happens for us. In the words of the song "Nights in White Satin" by the Moody Blues, one of my favorite musical groups, "Just what you want to be, you will be in the end." The problem is that we have been headed individually and collectively to what we thought we wanted to be, but this is not who our spirits *came here to be.*

Take your personal power back. "Know thyself" and trust in who you are in God. This will transform your fear. We are being given the opportunity to stay open-hearted and come from love, compassion, and empathy, versus being in fear and contraction. The power of choice lies within each of us. Choose wisely.

MAIN TAKEAWAY

You have the power to determine how you see things and how you respond to fear.

Feel into the fear that just came up within you.
Ask what it wants to teach you and just be present with it.

AFTERWORD

M ost of us had an idea where we *thought* this journey of life was taking us, and this has likely been at least partially uprooted by the coronavirus crisis, probably significantly. The word "thought" is italicized because I want to emphasize that we actually didn't know where life was taking us — we only thought we knew. An uncertain future has revealed the falsity of believing we were on a certain track, and some are handling this fear of the unknown better than others.

There are gifts inherent in every crisis. Everything in life can and is meant to be used for a higher understanding. A large gift of the coronavirus crisis is to help us realize that we have an addiction to and a belief in what is false. Sometimes people with an addiction voluntarily go to treatment, but often an intervention is required by loved ones. Because we are collectively in this together, God and the Universe are forcing an intervention because we are headed off a cliff. How we have been treating each other, our spirits, and the planet isn't sustainable. We need a radical course alteration.

196 A BOOK ON FEAR

We have come to this point as a result of the combination of our individual choices along with our giving our power away to others who have made choices, many of which we are not aware of, that are not in the best interest of everyone as one humanity. With the coronavirus and likely with additional things that will be revealed, God is opening the curtain to show us what these choices have created.

This not God's retribution or some kind of punishment since God is Love. We are just being shown how out of balance we have been, and how we have strayed from what we have asked for individually and collectively at a spirit level, which is to evolve, learn, and remember and help others do the same. In so many ways we have been lost in an illusion of what we thought was worthwhile and essential. Can each of us now be the frog waking up and jumping out of the pot before we are collectively boiled alive?

Once we fully understand the consequences of the choices we have made and the choices that have been made for us without our consent, we have the opportunity to choose a different path that leads to a different outcome. Will we continue to choose fear and to give our power away? Will we continue to choose technology as our master and live in a virtual sterile AI world that is soulless and devoid of everything that brings us joy as divine beings operating in an incredible natural world? Is loss of our humanness and our freedom the price for giving the *appearance* of suppression of our fear? For it would only be an appearance, as the fear would still be there but just held down.

Or will we choose a reality where we take a deep dive into what's causing our fear and choose a different way? Will we look at what's behind the curtain? Choosing a non-fear-based reality doesn't mean that with a situation like the coronavirus, we don't take precautions and prepare where needed. But it means we take a much broader perspective and envision a different way *while* we are dealing with the reality of the current situation. In God all things are possible, and we only need to ask for and envision it. There are so many solutions and potential outcomes we haven't even imagined yet because we are not open to seeing them, as fear prevents that.

What is the virus teaching and showing us, and how can we come out of this with more unity and love-based understanding and practices, versus more separation? For a belief in separation has led us to the cliff.

As the curtain is opened, we may experience a wide range of emotions, especially fear and anger. Discernment instead of judgment will be critical. Judgment condemns both the action and the person or authority committing that action. Discernment condemns only the action. We stay open-hearted, which gives us a non-fear-based perspective to know the right decisions to take in response to that action.

Staying open-hearted and in love and compassion is also important for several other reasons. Albert Einstein helped us understand: "No problem can be solved from the level of consciousness that created it." Our world can't be healed using the means of the world. Only by raising our perspective to one of unity and love can solutions present themselves.

Second, just as we do with our individual fear when it arises in us, we need to embrace and send healing energy to the whole body of God, especially authorities and individuals who are making choices that aren't best for the whole. Jesus made it very clear. He communicated many teachings through parables, but these were steps on the ladder to a higher truth which he stated unequivocally: "Love our neighbor as ourself, love our enemies, and love God with all of our heart, mind, and soul."

We are one body of God, one family. If we hate a part of that body, we are hating ourselves. Similar to the fear that arises in us individually and is our teacher, what are these other parts of God, which are taking actions not in the best interest of the whole, trying to teach us? When we stay in love and compassion, we will understand a great deal and take a large leap in our personal evolution. Individually and collectively, we will create the Kingdom of God that Jesus said is within us and we can have right now.

We will also discover the gifts that we have been given and that we are meant to use in service to the world. Envision yourself as a clear vessel through which God works to bless others.

Similar to the caterpillar in the cocoon or a forest which is decomposing, the next few years are a time of great change and may be messy. This is how transformation happens. We may not feel as if we have any footing or there is anything familiar to which we can turn. Maybe we can control some things, and maybe we can figure some things out. Maybe not. Be comfortable with a flexible belief system, for this is how we can flow with the fear and navigate the waters going forward. The ego mind always needs some kind of answer, but sometimes accepting we don't have the answer *is* the answer. This will place us in a beautiful and peace-filled state of non-judgment of ourselves and others.

And always come back to this when fear rises up within you. Life goes on. Even when the world appears to be breaking down around you and everything you have known as real is being challenged, the sun still rises and sets every day. The birds still sing, the tides still come in and out, and every moment we take a breath. As I write this, the daffodils are coming up like they do every spring. They are beautiful reminders to me of the cycles of life and renewal. Our dogs are staying close to me, expecting their daily walk. They don't know that the world appears to be crashing. They just want to be fed, walked, and to give and receive love. Pretty nice and simple, as in how God created it. This is what I deem as essential.

We can take comfort in these things because they are eternal and real. They remind us of what is eternal and real within ourselves.

Many blessings and much love to you during these life-changing times.

Larry

For more information on
Lawrence Doochin, please visit

lawrencedoochin.com

Made in United States
Troutdale, OR
06/29/2023

10881986R00127